Islamist Influence in Hollywood

Islamist Influence in HOLLYWOOD

By Deborah Weiss, Esq.

War is peace. Freedom is slavery. Ignorance is strength.
– George Orwell

Politics is downstream from culture.
– Andrew Breitbart

Center for Security Policy Press

ISBN-13: 978-1985619043
ISBN-10: 198561904

The Center for Security Policy
Washington, D.C.
Phone: 202-835-9077
Email: info@SecureFreedom.org
For more information, visit SecureFreedom.org

Book design by Bravura Books

CONTENTS

FOREWORD

The Center for Security Policy's Civilization Jihad Reader series documents the extent of the Muslim Brotherhood's 50-year-long *and ongoing*, stealthy assault on the pillars of American society. This body of work now features 12 highly informative, rigorously documented and in-depth treatments of manifestations of this phenomenon, including: Sharia-supremacism (*Shariah: The Threat to America*); "interfaith dialogue" (*Bridge Building to Nowhere*); political warfare (*Star Spangled Shariah*); the Red-Green axis (*Team Jihad*); official "willful blindness" (*See No Shariah*); the assault on the Constitution and the judiciary (*Shariah in American Courts*); and Brotherhood front groups (*CAIR is Hamas* and *Hamas, CAIR and the Muslim Brotherhood*).

Now, Deborah Weiss, Esq. – an internationally recognized expert on free speech and efforts by Sharia-supremacists and others to suppress it, the subject of her previous CSP monograph, *The Organization of Islamic Cooperation's Jihad on Free Speech* – brings us a shocking exposé on the extent of Muslim Brotherhood influence inside Hollywood and America's film-making industry more generally. Operating as always behind the cover of its many front groups, the Brotherhood has achieved a level of control over what we watch on our electronic devices, movie screens, and televisions that is largely unknown by the vast majority of consumers of such fare.

As Ms. Weiss warns in her introduction to *Islamist Influence in Hollywood*: "The West is in a war with the Global Jihad Movement. It is primarily a war of ideas, and the mind is the battlefield. Muslim Brotherhood front-groups have targeted Hollywood as one of many vehicles through which to conduct its civilization jihad."

The civilization jihad, as explained in the Brotherhood's own, secret 1991 *Explanatory Memorandum*, is a non-violent – or, more accurately, *pre-violent* – campaign waged from bases of operation the organization has established throughout American society. Its explicit purpose is "destroying Western Civilization from within and sabotaging its miserable house by their hands [i.e., those of non-Muslim Americans]." This alarming mission statement makes clear that the Brotherhood's purpose is seditious and that it has a sophisticated understanding of how to go about taking us down. Most

Americans, *and especially the vast majority of their elected representatives,* are clueless on both scores.

Ms. Weiss' latest monograph is a most helpful *and necessary* corrective to this national lack of situational awareness concerning the Muslim Brotherhood's efforts to use the popular culture for such nefarious purposes. She exposes both the Brotherhood's nefarious actions, as well as the willful or unwitting complicity of all-too-many Hollywood moguls, directors, producers, screen writers and actors.

In fact, this meticulously researched monograph should serve as a blueprint for a significant course-correction not just for the entertainment industry with respect to the Muslim Brotherhood and other Sharia-supremacists. It should encourage a similar response by U.S. homeland security, intelligence, and law enforcement agencies charged with monitoring and countering domestic subversion.

After all, as Ms. Weiss demonstrates, the Muslim Brotherhood is a past-master at executing an anti-constitutional Sharia agenda through influence operations that subtly affect attitudes, feelings, thoughts "and ultimately the decisions and behavior of the target audience." Its three most important and mutually reinforcing tactics are censorship, disinformation and infiltration.

Brotherhood censorship in Hollywood increasingly ensures that no negative portrayal of Islam or Muslims is allowed to reach the "silver screen." Disinformation inserts false and misleading material and images into American films that serve to obscure the character and implications of Sharia for freedom and people who prize it.

Finally, Sharia-adherent Muslims are encouraged to enter the Hollywood filmmaking industry to achieve the sort of penetration and influence that the Muslim Brotherhood has sought in other pillars of American society. (The latter includes, notably, the way entry-level Muslim candidates have been groomed to run for political office.) HAMAS/Brotherhood groups such as the Council on American Islamic Relations (CAIR) and the Muslim Public Affairs Council (MPAC) have operated at the forefront of this effort in Hollywood literally for decades. Today, their staff members and associates are accepted as influential "consultants" throughout the film industry.

None of this would be possible without massive funding from Muslim sources and those they dominate, such as the United Nations-sponsored Alliance of Civilizations (AoC). The AoC has pumped millions of dollars into the effort to whitewash the truth of the global Islamic jihad, vilify Israel and Jews, and deceive gullible American viewers across a span of media technologies. Film festivals, Lalaland *Iftar* dinners, production companies and demonstrations all play a reinforcing role.

We hope that this new monograph can play a role in Hollywood, too – by exposing Americans to the shocking reality that they are being insidiously manipulated by the popular culture, an influence vector against which they are unlikely to be steeled. With the benefit of the evidence Deborah Weiss has marshaled and the insights she sensibly draws from it, our consumers can begin to exercise a salutary influence: rewarding and otherwise reinforcing those in the entertainment industry who are willing to tell the truth about Sharia and its champions.

Frank J. Gaffney, Jr.
President and CEO
Center for Security Policy
February 14, 2018

WE ARE AT WAR

The West is in a war with the Global Jihad Movement. It is primarily a war of ideas, and the mind is the battlefield. Muslim Brotherhood front-groups have targeted Hollywood as one of many vehicles through which to conduct its civilization jihad. That they have left no sphere of society untouched and no stone unturned is evidence of the thoroughness of their strategy to subvert western society from within. Islamist influence in Hollywood abounds, and it would be a grave mistake to assume that it is innocuous. Its impact will have a reverberating and deleterious effect for generations to come unless it is acknowledged, confronted and countered.

CHAPTER 1

Hollywood as a Target For Civilization Jihad and Influence Operations: Background Information

Jihad Does Not Require Violence

Having witnessed the rise of the Islamic State in Iraq & al-Sham (ISIS – since 2014, renamed simply Islamic State – IS), Al-Nusra, Boko Haram, Hamas and Hizballah in the Middle East, and having experienced 9/11, 7/7, Charlie Hebdo, Paris, Orlando, San Bernardino and the increase of IS-inspired terrorist attacks in the West, it would be hard for Americans in 2017 not to have some idea of what the word "jihad" means.

Literally translated from Arabic, the word "jihad" means "striving" or "struggle."[1] In the context of Islam, it means "holy war" against infidels or non-Muslims to further Islam's cause. [2] Most people understandably associate the word jihad with Islamic terrorism.

Many people, however, don't realize that jihad does not necessarily require violence. Non-violent or pre-violent "stealth jihad" (also called "civilization jihad") serves the same purpose as violent jihad: to conquer infidel territory and replace all man-made systems with Islamic law, known as "shariah."[3]

Islam is a Political Religion

Islam, properly understood, is not simply a religion as we understand religion in the West. In fact, Muslim authorities and even the textbooks used in American *madrassas* (schools), explain that Islam is not a 'religion.' Rather, it is a whole way of life that includes judicial, military, political, financial, and educational components, in addition to its religious aspect. It is, in effect, a totalitarian political ideology that seeks to impose its will on people of all faiths, both Muslim and non-Muslim alike.[4] Indeed, the literal translation of Islam in Arabic is "submission," not "peace" as apologists would have you believe.[5]

As a political religion, Islam's two main goals are the re-establishment of an Islamic Caliphate and the worldwide implementation of Islamic law.[6] Those who aspire to establish an "Islamic State" do not intend this state to be confined to a limited geographic territory like Saudi Arabia or Iran. They want the entire world to consist of only one nation – the nation of Islam.[7] This state would be ruled by a Caliph, and shariah would be administered by the government through force of law. Adherence to it would not be volitional.[8]

Shariah institutionalizes discrimination.[9] Under shariah, Muslims are favored over non-Muslims, men are favored over women, and homosexuality is strictly forbidden. Shariah rejects both freedom of speech and freedom of religion.[10] Its criminal punishments are cruel and unusual, and there is no due process of law. Therefore, many aspects of shariah are anti-Constitutional.[11] In its entirety, shariah is anathema to human rights. [12]

While shariah allows "People of the Book," (meaning primarily Christians and Jews), to practice their religion to a limited extent under certain conditions, infidels do not have any rights independent from what Muslims choose to grant them, and these rights can be retracted at any time.[13] Those who are not Christians or Jews have no rights at all. [14]

As a political religion, Islam seeks to ever expand its dominance: its ideology, its territory and its political power.[15] And, like other totalitarian ideologies, it has numerous strategies and tactics with which to achieve its goals.

Jihad (both violent and stealth) is a main method to further the cause of Islam and is mandated by shariah. The Muslim Brotherhood and its affiliates wage jihad largely through stealthy means. [16] But make no mistake about it: the Muslim Brotherhood and its front-groups have the exact same goals as Al-Qaeda and other Islamic terrorist groups. They differ only in their tactics and timing.

The Muslim Brotherhood In America

The Muslim Brotherhood was created in Egypt in 1928, after the fall of the Ottoman Empire.[17] The Brotherhood lays out its strategic plan explicitly in the 1991 Explanatory Memorandum Strategy for North America. [18] Notably, this document was admitted into evidence without objection from the defense, during the 2008 Holy Land Foundation (HLF) HAMAS terror funding trial, the largest terror financing trial in the history of the United States. [19]

The Memo includes extensive explanations of the tactics to be used by the Muslim Brotherhood to insinuate itself into every aspect of society and "settle Islam" in the West for the purposes of achieving its ultimate goal of world domination. [20]

Some of the tactics include, but are not limited to: infiltration into all aspects of society, disinformation campaigns, influence operations, deception, censorship, perception management and the formation of "coalitions" with "progressive" groups in every area of life. [21] Muslim Brotherhood front groups fight to dominate the information battlespace, indoctrinate various societal sectors and take control of societal narratives. This is evident across the interfaith community, college campuses, mainstream media, government, and yes, even Hollywood.

At the end of the Memorandum is a list of 29 organizations which the Muslim Brotherhood considers its affiliates. [22] They often work together toward shared goals. Some of these organizations and others of their ilk are working fastidiously to persuade Hollywood to do their bidding for them by censoring the truth and creating false narratives. The Memorandum explains that:

> "[T]he Ikhwan must understand that their work in America is a kind of grand jihad in eliminating and destroying the Western civilization from within and sabotaging its miserable house by *their hands* and the hands of the believers so that it is eliminated and Allah's religion is made victorious over all other religions."[23]

In analyzing this statement, it should be noted that sabotage by "their hands" refers to the hands of infidels and the hands of "the believers" refers to the hands of shariah-adherent Muslims. In short, the Memo makes clear that Muslims won't be able to destroy America by themselves. They will enlist the aid of American non-Muslims who will unwittingly contribute to the death of their own freedom and commit suicide to the American way of life.

This monograph will review some of the Muslim organizations that are waging influence operations in Hollywood in order to change our culture and provide false or misleading information about Islam, terrorism and jihad. The end goal of these groups is to blind Americans to the truth about the Global Jihad Threat, because without the ability to properly identify our enemies, we are powerless to defeat them, thereby providing jihadists with a strategic advantage.

What Is an Influence Operation?

Certainly Muslim Americans have the same right as others to produce, direct and appear in films. But that doesn't mean that we should be unaware that many Muslim organizations with a subversive political agenda are producing films as part of a larger Islamic supremacist mission for Da'wa (Islamic propaganda).[24]

An influence operation is the purposeful effort to gain positions of power and disseminate information in a way that will influence the feelings, thoughts, attitudes, and ultimately the decisions and behaviors of the target audience.[25] In this case, Islamic groups with a supremacist political ideology are injecting themselves into the film-making industry largely to control the mainstream narrative on Islam, influence public discourse, and ultimately impact decision-makers in policy positions, national security and law enforcement.

Islamic supremacists working in the film industry have focused primarily on three tactics: 1) censorship, 2) disinformation, and 3) infiltration.

Censorship attempts aim to purge all images, storylines (fact or fiction), and language that sheds Islam or Muslims in a negative light. More specifically, as this monograph will delineate, Muslim groups are trying to dissociate Islam from terrorism in the minds of the American audience. Toward this end, they lobby producers, script-writers and others in the entertainment industry to alter their plots and characters, and ensure that the "villains" of the story will be confined to non-Muslims and exclude Muslims.

Further, they work to ensure that Muslim characters inserted into movies will be shown in a positive light. Mostly, they seek to demonstrate that regardless of ideology, Muslims are not more likely to commit terrorism than non-Muslims, that Muslims have the same values as Jews and Christians, and that American-Muslims are just like everyone else (meaning American non-Muslims). In other words, they attempt to conceal the principles inherent in Islam that mandate discrimination against women, persecution of non-Muslims, restraints on freedom of speech and religion, as well as Islam's foundational human rights antipathy. They want Americans to remain ignorant or willfully blind to the cruel and inhumane criminal punishments that are part and parcel of Islam, and to remain uneducated regarding the true nature of Islam and the obligation for jihad.

Therefore, some Muslim organizations provide pre-written storylines for Hollywood. Others offer awards for those who portray Muslims in positive roles. Several offer "consulting services" or "educational programs" on Islam that disseminate falsehoods, half-truths or pro-Islam-biased information.

One of the goals of providing this disinformation is to disarm the public and America's national security apparatus. The famous Chinese Military General, Sun Tzu said that if you want to win a war, you must know two things: you must know who you are and you must know who the enemy is. You must be able to identify your enemy and name him by name. You must understand him as he understands himself: his goals, motivations and strategies. [26] Absent this, your chances for winning a war are drastically reduced. We are not in a War on Terror, for terrorism is simply a tactic. [27] We are in a war against the Global Jihad Movement. [28] The "kinetic" or military aspect is only one aspect of the war. It is primarily a War of Ideas, and we ignore the ideological component at our own peril. [29]

Far-leftists, the uninformed, and the naïve often buy into [30] Islamic supremacist cries of "bigotry" and "Islamophobia" [31] in response to government's passage of anti-terrorism legislation. [32] Shariah-adherent Muslims who hold the same religious views that fuel terrorist acts at home and abroad are couching themselves as "victims" in order to gain sympathy for their anti-freedom goals, such as censorship of free speech. [33] To the degree that we accept the victimhood narrative and acquiesce to it, or "go along to get along," we endanger not only our national security, but ultimately our freedom.

The best way supremacist organizations can boost their political agenda in Hollywood is to encourage young Muslims to enter film-related professions, including film-production and script-writing. That's why several organizations are now offering scholarships for Muslims who enter related fields, sometimes placing ideological or organization affiliation requirements as pre-requisites to qualify for funding. Some also offer Muslims networking opportunities with Hollywood professionals, mentoring programs or professional advice to give Hollywood-minded Muslims a leg up.

Muslim Brotherhood front groups and other Islamic supremacist groups are producing films and interacting with Hollywood elites in order to affect the mindset, not only of Hollywood professionals, but the culture at large. This effectively constitutes hostile intent that runs counter to American interests and advantages our Islamic supremacist enemies.

The Role of Hollywood

In June of 2016, America was mourning the results of the deadly jihadist attack on "the Pulse," an LGBT club in Orlando, Florida. It resulted in 49 dead and over 50 others injured, many of whom were fighting for their lives with critical injuries. The jihadi attack was launched merely hours before CBS was to air the 70th Anniversary of the Tony Awards.[34]

Yet, Hollywood, which has strong ties to the political left and the LGBT community in particular,[35] mischaracterized the attack, limiting it to nothing more than a "hate crime" against the LGBT community and steadfastly refusing to acknowledge the importance of the massacre as a terrorist act. Accordingly, they responded with calls for unity and love rather than an effective strategy to defeat the Global Jihad Movement. The LGBT movement toed the leftist political line demanding "gay dignity" and stiffer gun control laws as solutions to the problem.[36]

A proper analysis, however, would not have focused solely on the target of the attack (the LGBT community) and the method of killing (guns), but would have emphasized the clearly stated motives of the perpetrator (his allegiance to ISIS). Yet much of the media, Hollywood, and "progressive" politicians continued to speak out in accordance with what they speculated or wished the perpetrator's motives to be, ignoring the jihadist's plainly stated words. [37]

Unfortunately, the left, including Hollywood has been influenced by the Muslim Brotherhood narrative. Even worse, Hollywood has been complicit in contributing to it, whether knowingly or unwittingly.

Everyone who has children knows that media – whether it's new media like Facebook and Twitter, or traditional media like television and Hollywood movies – influences young minds and helps shape their worldviews. [38] It is, therefore, no coincidence that Muslim Brotherhood operatives have been targeting Hollywood for manipulation.

The independent film industry has additionally been a target for influence operations, as many writers and producers in the business believe that this sector is initially easier to break into and will ultimately be followed by changes to mainstream movies.

Ridley Scott, a three-time Academy Award-nominated British producer and director who has made numerous successful box office hits including *Thelma and Louise, Black Hawk Down,* and *Gladiator,* believes that one way to effectuate change is by filming in North Africa and the Middle East. He explains, "The change will come from independent filmmaking, but audiences have to be there. Because once that happens, financiers of bigger and bigger budget films will say, 'We can actually do business here.' "[39]

CHAPTER 2

THE COUNCIL ON AMERICAN-ISLAMIC RELATIONS

CAIR's True Colors

Let's take CAIR (Council on American Islamic Relations) for example. CAIR holds itself out as a Muslim Civil Rights organization, but in fact, it is a Muslim Brotherhood front group with terror ties. [40]

Founded in 1994, it spawned out of the Islamic Association of Palestine and Hamas, both Department of State-designated terrorist organizations. It's intended to promote Hamas' agenda while managing perceptions for the Muslim Brotherhood to an unwitting audience. In effect, it serves as the propaganda wing for Hamas.[41]

It was an unindicted co-conspirator in the Holy Land Foundation trial, the largest terror financing trial in the history of the U.S.[42] It has numerous terror ties, not just a few bad apples as its leadership would have us believe. Indeed, several of CAIR's former leadership, board members, advisors and speakers are either sitting in jail on terror-related convictions, have affiliations with terrorist organizations, or show support for those convicted.[43] Virtually all of them support Hamas and Hizballah[44] and CAIR itself is a designated terrorist organization in the UAE.[45]

Inferring intent by its patterns of conduct, it is clear that CAIR has three main goals: to protect Islam from so-called "defamation" (meaning to silence all criticism of Islam and Muslims), to obtain special preferences for Muslims in the workplace, and to hamper American national security efforts.[46]

As previously indicated, Muslim Brotherhood front groups operate in all sectors of society to influence policies, viewpoints, power structures, and to control the flow of information. CAIR in particular has an expansive influence operations agenda, infiltrating government entities, interfaith groups, academia, media, and Hollywood.

CAIR's Influence In Hollywood

CAIR has been very effective in persuading Hollywood to censor itself and alter film scripts to fit its narratives. Nihad Awad, founding member of CAIR and current Executive Director of CAIR National boasts in his bio that he has successfully negotiated with Hollywood to combat "negative stereotypes of Muslims" in various movies.[47]

In a 2010 speech, Awad falsely claimed that one Hollywood company alone created 800 films about Muslims in the prior three decades, presenting Muslims and Arabs from "an Israeli point of view."[48] This is the same Nihad Awad who has openly declared that he is a "supporter of the Hamas movement."[49] But in fact, there had not been any Hollywood production company that created that many films of any kind during that time period, with or without a negative portrayal of Muslims.[50]

Unfortunately, Hollywood producers, directors and screen-writers have in large measure, capitulated to CAIR's demands. Following are some examples of CAIR's pressure and influence in Hollywood.

Example #1: Movie, *The Sum of All Fears*, produced by Paramount Pictures, 2002[51]

This film was based on a thriller authored by Tom Clancy, and starred Ben Affleck. The original plot portrayed Islamic terrorists shooting down an Israeli jet over Syria which was carrying nuclear weapons.

CAIR complained that the film engaged in "negative stereotyping of Muslims." For two whole years prior to the film's release, CAIR lobbied the producer and director, pressuring them to change the characters. In fact, the producer stated that he was getting complaints even before the script was completed.

Eventually, the director changed the villains in the film from Muslims to Australian neo-Nazis. As a result of the change, many who saw the movie said that the film's plot made no sense.

Example #2: Movie, *True Lies*, produced by 20th Century Fox, 1994[52]

This film starred Arnold Schwarzenegger and Jamie Lee Curtis. It was about Islamic terrorists and a spy with an unfaithful wife.

CAIR repeatedly demanded meetings with the producers, complaining that the plot constituted "negative stereotyping." CAIR's demands were declined. Consequently, CAIR organized events to protest the film and issued leaflets to movie-goers on the subject of Islam.

Under ratcheted up pressure, eventually 20th Century Fox agreed to include a disclaimer in the film, stating that it is a work of fiction and does not represent the actions or beliefs of any particular religion.

Example #3: Movie, *The Siege*, produced by 20th Century Fox, 1998[53]

This was a fictional film about Islamic terrorists intent on destroying New York City. CAIR met with the producers prior to the film's release to demand changes in the script. Minor adjustments were made, but the overall plot remained the same.

Upon the film's release, CAIR held a press conference criticizing the portrayal of Islamic terrorists. CAIR's press release stated that the film would cause many who see the movie to "view the next Muslim or Arab they meet with increased suspicion and hostility." Additionally, CAIR organized numerous activities to undermine the film. The activities included handing out "Siege Campaign Kits" to movie-goers, holding discussion panels and running newspaper ads opposing it, and holding open house events at mosques to try to show Islam in a positive light.

Example #4: Movie, *Kingdom of Heaven*, produced by 20th Century Fox, 2005[54]

This Hollywood film starred Liam Neeson and Orlando Bloom. It was about the Crusades and the battle for Jerusalem.

The production company, 20th Century Fox, already had a history of problems with CAIR. For past film productions, CAIR had issued action alerts to its members who then sent a barrage of complaints to the producers.

In an attempt to ward off additional run-ins with CAIR, the producers of Kingdom of Heaven hired Hamid Dabashia, an Iranian-American Muslim consultant whose views are anti-Israel and anti-American. The producers also gave CAIR a special pre-screening of the film prior to its release. As a result of CAIR's feedback, the producers wound up editing out scenes from the film script prior to its release.

In the end, the movie depicted the Christians as murderers and hypocrites and the Muslims as morally superior. This final version constituted CAIR's idea of a "balanced" portrayal of the Crusades.

Example #5: Movie, *Executive Decision,* produced by Warner Brothers, 1996[55]

This Hollywood film starring Kurt Russell, Steven Seagal and Halle Berry was about Islamic terrorists who hijacked a 747 airplane on the way from Greece to Washington, D.C., and the executive decision required to safeguard the plane's passengers.

Despite the fact that nothing in the film stated or implied that all Muslims are terrorists, CAIR insisted that merely portraying Islamic terrorists negatively stereotyped Muslims.

Still, the original version of the film was released in the United States without edits. The German and U.K. versions, however, cut a scene where the jihadist was praying and another scene where a knife was used during the course of an attack. Additionally, when the Arabic language version was dubbed into German, the translation omitted all use of the words "Allah" and "Islam."[56]

In 2011, Warner Brothers released a Blu-ray version, which removed several scenes showing the Qu'ran or of the jihadist praying. [57]

Additionally, the 2014 U.S. TV version of the film made dubbed changes into its soundtrack, replacing the words "Allah" and "infidel" with "God" and "enemy" respectively, among other language changes. Further, the terrorist's country of origin (Algeria, which is a Muslim majority country), was suddenly omitted. Notably, these changes remained on channels dedicated to movies without commercial interruption, which usually don't make edits or cuts to the original scripts. [58]

Though there is no public claim of credit by CAIR for these specific changes (nor does CAIR operate in some of the relevant countries), it is clear that these changes were made in order not to "offend" Muslims. [59]

Example #6: Movie, *Rules of Engagement,* produced by Paramount Pictures, 2015[60]

This film was about a Marine Colonel who ordered his men to fire into a crowd that was descending upon the U.S. Embassy in Yemen because he believed people in the crowd were armed. The film includes the story of the Colonel's subsequent trial for giving the order to fire.[61]

CAIR issued a press release arguing that the film "seems to justify the killing of Muslim men, women and even children" and provides "a very negative and inaccurate image of Muslims and Islamic beliefs."[62]

CAIR asserted that the film was made in "cooperation with the Department of Defense." Accordingly, CAIR called on the Secretary of Defense to change the Pentagon's policy to ensure that it does not "associate itself with anti-Muslim stereotyping in the film industry."[63] Fortunately, both the Pentagon and the producers stuck to their guns, so to speak, and refused to alter the film in capitulation to CAIR.[64]

Example #7: Islamic terrorism portrayed by CBS[65]

CAIR-New York is one of the most aggressive CAIR chapters. In 2001, three months prior to 9/11,[66] it placed a demand on CBS to stop airing all films, TV and radio shows on Islamic terrorism, whether they were fact of fiction, stating that these "defame" Muslims and promote anti-Muslim stereotypes. It argued that airing these would cause hostility leading to discrimination, and subject innocent little children to harassment in schools and on playgrounds.

In furtherance of this goal, CAIR-NY also started a petition protesting CBS and calling for a boycott of all CBS stations on TV and radio, in both the news and entertainment divisions. It also worked to boycott CBS' advertisers. CAIR-NY threatened that if its demands were not met, it would make sure that CBS productions would be precluded from entering any of the then-54 Muslim majority countries that comprised the Organization of Islamic Conference (OIC, later the Organization of Islamic Cooperation).[67]

CAIR-NY also wanted several Chuck Norris films to be withheld from air as well as the film *Not without My Daughter*, starring Sally Fields. The latter was a fictitious story about an American woman who married an Iranian Muslim with whom she later had a daughter. After a trip visiting the husband's family in Iran, the husband refused to return to America or permit his wife to take their daughter back. The film portrays the trials and tribulations the wife endured in order to leave the Islamic Republic of Iran with her daughter.

Additional films that CAIR-NY demanded be withheld from the air included, *The Agency, The Path to Paradise,* and *Terrorist Trial: The Unites States vs. Salim Ajam.*

At the time, the pressure yielded some results, as CBS informed the LA Times in July of 2001, that in an upcoming film on terrorism it would remove all depictions of Muslims.

Example #8: TV series, *24*, produced by Fox, 2001-2010[68]

CAIR has also been active in trying to censor television shows that portray Islam or Muslims in a negative light.

24 was a case in point. It was a popular TV series produced by Fox and eventually syndicated worldwide. The first show aired in November 2001 and subsequently, approximately 192 episodes were shown over an eight-season period. The series was nominated for scores of Emmy Awards and won several awards including Best Drama Series at the Golden Globe Awards, and Outstanding Drama Series at the Emmy's.

The storyline was about a counter-terrorism agent who tried to thwart cyber, biological, chemical, and terrorist attacks. The series portrayed villains from a wide range of religious and ethnic backgrounds including, but not limited to, American, German, Muslim and Russian.

In January, 2005, a *24* episode portrayed a Muslim family as part of a sleeper cell. Two days later, CAIR met with Fox to complain about Fox's portrayal of Muslims as terrorists, claiming it will cause "anti-Muslim prejudice."

Fox caved in to CAIR's demands and cut out of its series several scenes that portrayed Muslims negatively. Fox additionally permitted CAIR to air public service announcements (PSAs) on its station using Muslims of various ethnicities stating, "I am an American Muslim."

Subsequently, as a result of yet another run-in with CAIR regarding *24*, Fox issued a statement emphasizing the fact that the villains come from a variety of backgrounds, that the TV show is fiction, and that Fox assumes that people can distinguish fiction from reality.

Example #9: TV series, *Alice In Saudi Arabia,* produced by ABC, 2014

Alice in Saudi Arabia was a TV series written by an American woman who served in the U.S. Army as an Arabic linguist, trained to support NSA missions in the Middle East.[69] The story line was about a mixed-race American girl whose extended family took her to Saudi Arabia where she was forced to live as a veiled Muslim woman. According to the writer, the purpose of the series was to demonstrate the complexities of the Middle East and to move the audience toward a more Muslim-sympathetic point of view.[70]

But this wasn't sufficient for CAIR and its allies. The pilot was ready for release on ABC. However, CAIR and the American-Arab Anti-Discrimination League (AADC) had gotten hold of an advance copy of the script and launched a campaign to prevent the TV series from airing. They asserted that the series engaged in "stereotyping" of Muslims and Arabs.[71] As a result of the pressure, ABC made a decision to drop the show prior to airing, never giving it a chance. Both CAIR and the AADC lauded the decision.[72]

Example #10: Documentary, *Honor Diaries,* produced by Ayaan Hirsi Ali and Raphael Shore et al, 2013

While American feminists whine about men who compliment their legs in the workplace or hold doors open for them to enter buildings, women and girls in Muslim countries are suffering extreme violence and discrimination on a regular, systematic and institutionalized basis.[73] Over 200 million girls and women living today have suffered female genital mutilation (FGM), most of whom reside in the Middle East and Africa.[74] Millions of Muslim girls are forced into "marriage" at a young age[75] to men old enough to be their fathers or grandfathers. These "marriages" are really sex slavery and rape, committed with the consent of the girl's parents, but absent the consent of the "bride." Though many Muslim countries have laws stating the legal age of marriage is 13 or 15,[76] in Islam itself, girls can get "married" at age 6 and consummate their marriages as young as age 9, based on the example of the Muslim Prophet Mohammad's marriage to his child bride, Aisha.[77] Using Mohammad's conduct as the role model, religious authorities often push for their countries to lower the legal age for child marriage.

Additionally, in Islam, the female carries the "honor" of the family, and it is the men who must guard it. Shariah encourages violence against women who violate Islam's rules. This is further sanctioned and encouraged by legislation in Muslim majority countries. Thousands of young women and girls are murdered every year by their fathers, mothers and brothers for having "dishonored" their families.[78] This dishonor can be deemed to have been perpetrated for merely removing their hijabs and revealing their hair, wearing short-sleeved shirts, talking to or dating men before marriage or doing anything that is too "westernized."[79] To make matters worse, these prohibitions are spreading to the West as the Muslim demographic grows through high birth rates and the influx of Muslim "refugees."

Honor Diaries, produced by Ayaan Hirsi Ali and Raphael Shore, among others,[80] is a documentary interviewing nine Muslim women of various backgrounds, to discuss the plight of Muslim women and girls under Islam. It is a human rights film, advocating for better treatment of women and girls, pushing for their right to be treated humanely and equally to men.[81]

The film was released on "International Women's Day," March 8, 2014. Many college campuses were scheduled to show the film.[82] However, CAIR protested the film and tried to get it shut down on college campuses. Apparently unable to find fault with the actual content of the film, CAIR claimed that the producers are "Islamophobic."[83]

Though many colleges showed the film despite the protests, CAIR was successful in getting a number of colleges to cancel or delay their screenings. For example, The State University of Oklahoma showed the film as part of "Sexual Violence Awareness Month" over the objections of CAIR, [84] but the University of Michigan in Dearborn and the University of Illinois in Chicago both cancelled the school's viewings. [85]

CAIR, one of the largest advocates for censorship of criticism of Islam, laughably had its spokesman, Ibrahim Hooper claim that it wasn't advocating for school censorship on shariah related problems. He advised colleges that want to raise awareness of violence against women and girls in Muslim countries, "'Don't cancel the event. Just cancel the film. Have the event to discuss domestic violence, female genital mutilation, whatever issue you want, but bring representatives of the Muslim community, bring other people, other experts, and have a legitimate discussion."[86]

In other words, to Ibrahim Hooper and CAIR, a discussion isn't "legitimate" unless it features apologists for Islam.

CAIR and Law Enforcement Training

CAIR has even protested the New York Police Department's use of the documentary, *The Third Jihad*, [87] which is about homegrown jihad and narrated by Dr. Zuhdi Jasser, President of the American Islamic-Forum for Democracy (AIFD) and a staunch advocate for separation of mosque and state. The film, which interviews numerous national security experts, was used in the NYPD's counter-terrorism training program. It made a disclaimer stating that the film is not about Islam, but about "the threat of radical Islam" and claimed that only a small fraction of Muslims constitute this threat.[88]

Nevertheless, CAIR protested the film, claiming it was "biased" and demanded an investigation of how such an "anti-Muslim" film could be used in NYPD training. Eventually, the NYPD capitulated to CAIR's pressure and dropped the film from its training program.[89] It's important to note that CAIR never claimed that the facts set forth in the film were inaccurate, and it is clear that CAIR's definition of "biased" includes true facts that reveal negative information about Islamic doctrine or groups.

CAIR also protested factually accurate films like the *The Rise of Al-Qaeda*, a documentary exhibited in the 9/11 Memorial Museum. [90] To its credit, the museum refused to remove the documentary from its exhibits.

Though neither of these films is a Hollywood movie specifically, CAIR's protests of factually accurate documentaries only underscores the point that CAIR's true motive is not to halt "negative stereotypes," but to prevent the public and law enforcement from knowing the truth.

Analysis:
CAIR Succeeds at Hollywood Censorship

Increasingly, instead of admitting it is acting on its own initiative, Hamas-linked CAIR is claiming it is merely responding to complaints by Muslim members or "community concerns.[91] Additionally, CAIR and other Islamic supremacist groups argue that films with "negative stereotypes" of Muslims will cause actual violence and potential "bullying of Muslim students" in addition to "anti-Muslim sentiment" [92]

This of course, is complete nonsense. Every individual is responsible for his or her own conduct. A comment, film, or television show cannot *cause* a person to behave in any particular way. Furthermore, there is no evidence whatsoever to support the claim that "negative" portrayals of Muslims or accurate portrayals of Islamic terrorists have increased violence against Muslims. CAIR and its sympathizers use this argument, linking words and images to violence in an attempt to legitimize censorship and the curtailment of speech. [93] Rather, all the evidence is to the contrary, demonstrating that where censorship and blasphemy laws abound, violence against those deemed non-shariah-adherent escalates rather than diminishes. [94] It is also important to note that CAIR has no compunction for the truth. To CAIR, "negative stereotypes of Muslims" may consist of nothing more than factual reporting.

It is important to understand that none of these films reviewed above portrayed or alleged that all Muslims are terrorists. But CAIR and its allies want no Muslims to be portrayed as terrorists. In fact, CAIR wants terrorists to be portrayed as anybody except Muslims. Additionally, CAIR is obviously not concerned with extending reciprocity for minority religions in Muslim majority countries. Accordingly, it does nothing to discourage the rampant negative stereotyping of Jews in the media of the OIC countries or in Arabic language media.[95]

CHAPTER 3

THE MUSLIM PUBLIC AFFAIRS COUNCIL

MPAC: Another Muslim Brotherhood Front Group

Like CAIR, the Muslim Public Affairs Council (MPAC) is also a Muslim Brotherhood affiliate.[96] Cloaked in the language of patriotism while "challenging our nation to live up to its values,"[97] MPAC has aligned with the far-left and the Democrat Party in America. It is active in the interfaith movement, Hollywood "engagement," and lobbying government. It has also started a "Safe Spaces Initiative."[98] In effect, it is a law enforcement evasion program, funneling would-be violent jihadists into programs training them how to channel their political and religious anger through non-violent means to achieve the same goals. MPAC also holds programs designed to place American-Muslims into internship positions on Capitol Hill and in Hollywood.[99]

Additionally, MPAC serves as an advocacy group, writing policy position papers on critical issues regarding national security and foreign policy. It regularly sponsors so-called anti-Islamophobia campaigns and campaigns to "empower" the Muslim community by helping Muslim-Americans to "engage in the civic process" by providing them with strategies to establish relationships with politicians on all levels: local, state and federal.[100]

MPAC, however, is far from the moderate organization that it holds itself out to be. It was established in 1988 by Muslim Brotherhood members who admired Hizballah.[101] One of MPAC's founders, Hassan Hathout, was a "close disciple" of Hassan al-Banna, the 20th century founder of the Muslim Brotherhood,[102] who was key in reviving jihad as an offensive strategy (rather than defensive) to further the spread of Islam.[103]

Unfortunately, the Obama Administration had close ties with MPAC, seemingly sympathetic with Islam generally, and Muslim Brotherhood groups in particular. Shockingly, the Obama State Department chose Salam al-Marayati, co-founder and President of MPAC[104] to represent the United States as part of its delegation at the Organization of Security and Cooperation in Europe (OSCE)'s human rights conference in 2012[105] despite the fact that al-Maryati has made overtly anti-Israel and antisemitic remarks.[106]

MPAC's Hollywood Bureau

Now, MPAC, through its "Hollywood Bureau," is trying to persuade Hollywood film-makers, writers, producers and actors to produce movies that depict Muslims and Islam with a positive slant. According to its website, the Bureau serves as a "bridge" connecting Hollywood with the Muslim community. Its stated goal is to increase the number of positive stories about Islam on television and in films, portraying Muslims in a more "humanizing" light. [107]

MPAC's Hollywood Bureau has developed several initiatives toward this end.

First, its staff regularly meets with film industry professionals to establish a relationship with those of influence in Hollywood so that they might have some sway. It serves as a "consultant" to studios and production companies on films and TV shows that pertain to Islam and other issues that have "an impact on the Muslim community." The Bureau posits that it "educates" film-makers and producers regarding "religious, political and cultural issues" of concern to the Muslim community to give them "context."[108]

Second, the Bureau hosts networking events encouraging Muslims to become involved in the film and TV industries. The events provide a forum in which young Muslims who aspire to become film-makers, producers or actors can mingle with those in the business and get advice on how to succeed in the entertainment field. [109] The events are not limited to Hollywood proper, but include networking opportunities with independent film producers. For example, in 2010, MPAC held a mixer in Los Angeles for its members and "Film Independent," a non-profit for indie films.[110] These events also provide "opportunities" for Hollywood professionals to pre-screen their work in front of Muslim audiences to get their input prior to public release.[111] MPAC "summits" target Muslim youth, encouraging them to enter fields of influence including policy, media and Hollywood. [112]

As MPAC's status increases, so does its influence in Hollywood and the film industry. For example, in January of 2017, MPAC was a corporate sponsor at the prestigious Sundance Film Festival, which is held every year in Park City, Utah [113] and was founded by Robert Redford. [114] MPAC was the first Muslim organization to participate in the Sundance Film Festival sponsorship, and as such included a panel titled, "Illuminating Muslim Narratives" as part of its program. MPAC claims support and "solidarity" with Hollywood notables participating in both the film festival and the anti-Trump women's rally (which MPAC lumped together on its website) including Chelsea Handler, Laura Dern, Benjamin Bratt and others. [115]

MPAC's Hollywood Bureau along with the MPAC Foundation, hosts an annual media awards gala dinner, which honors artists, authors, actors and others in the Hollywood film-making industry as well as the advertising industry with awards when they show Islam and Muslims from a more "humanizing" and "multi-dimensional" point of view. [116] The media award, "Honoring Voices of Courage and Conscience" [117] boasts of past winners including Alec Baldwin and Michael Moore. [118]

Analysis:
MPAC's Real Agenda

Despite MPAC claims to "educate" Hollywood professionals on Islam and related topics to provide a more "balanced and accurate" view, [119] by its own admission, what it really seeks is the portrayal of Islam and Muslims in a more positive light. Even MPAC's own website expressly asserts that its interest in Hollywood and film making is to influence and shape public opinion through media. [120]

MPAC, like other Islamic supremacist organizations, is trying to whitewash Islamic terrorism and censor the truth about jihadi motives in the public sphere. The Bureau's pre-screenings to Muslim audiences hardly constitute the "opportunities" for film-makers and producers that they purport to be. To the contrary, they are opportunities for MPAC to demand the scrubbing and censorship of Hollywood scenarios, plots, characters and story lines that run counter to the MPAC narrative.

As an Islamic supremacist organization and a Muslim Brotherhood affiliate, MPAC has an interest in Hollywood only to the extent that it can conduct influence operations within the entertainment industry and manipulate the final productions. Film producers, script writers and actors dare not portray Muslims in a negative light, entertain religious motivations for terrorist attacks, or communicate an accurate portrait of Islam's second class treatment of women and religious minorities. If they do, they will be subject to scorn, ridicule or worse. Those who refuse to follow the Bureau's advice are certain to be viewed as "Islamophobes," "racists" or "bigots." But Hollywood professionals who toe the Muslim Brotherhood narrative are bestowed with awards and acclaim.

CHAPTER 4

ADDITIONAL BOX OFFICE HITS THAT WHITEWASH OR GLORIFY ISLAMIC TERRORISM

Other films demonstrate how Hollywood is whitewashing, trivializing, minimizing and even glorifying Islamic terrorism. Following is a handful of box office hits that exemplify this point.

1) *Paradise Now* was directed by an Israeli born Palestinian glorified suicide bombing [121] and won a Golden Globe Award. [122] and was nominated for a Golden Globe Award, among others.[123]

2) The film *Munich*, a Dreamworks film written by Tony Kushner and directed by Steven Spielberg, made a moral equivalency between Israeli counterterrorism efforts and Palestinian terrorism.[124] It was nominated for several Academy Awards, Golden Globe Awards, and numerous other awards.[125]

3) *Syriana*, starring George Clooney, blames the US for the conduct of Islamic terrorists in the Middle East.[126] This film was produced by Participant Productions (discussed in more detail in the monograph's next section) and won an Oscar Award, a Golden Globe Award, a Screen Actors Guild Award and many other awards.[127]

CHAPTER 5

The United Nations Influences Hollywood: The Alliance of Civilizations Media Fund

The Alliance of Civilizations: A Pro-Islam Bent at the UN

The United Nations is notorious for its pro-Islam bent at the Human Rights Council and the General Assembly. Additionally, in 2005, at the initiative of Spain and Turkey, an organization named the Alliance of Civilizations (AoC) was formed within the United Nations. It was designated to explore and address the "roots of polarization between societies and cultures." In furtherance of its ultimate mission, the AoC acted as a "bridge-builder and convener....to promote trust and understanding .... particularly but not exclusively between Muslim and Western societies." [128]

The AoC Media Fund: Funding Pro-Islam Films

As part of the AoC's implementation plan, the AoC launched its Media Fund in January of 2008, [129] which also had a pro-Islam bent. It was co-founded by Queen Noor of Jordan[130] whose husband, King Hussein, insisted that he was a direct descendant of the Muslim Prophet Muhammad.[131]

The fund was to be the first of its kind, a mega-media production company intent on "normalizing" those who are otherwise "stereotyped" in the media. It would focus on production, distribution and promotion of cross-cultural and "religious" content in film, television and news media. [132] Queen Noor stated that the fund's purpose was to "support the production and distribution of films that entertain as well as enlighten."[133]

Reportedly, the Media Fund had an initial financial investment of 10 million dollars with a target goal of 100 million dollars and was an independently incorporated non-profit held under the auspices of the AoC. It established numerous "partnerships" with leaders in the entertainment and new media industries as well as the United Nations.[134] According to CAIR's press center, the fund was designed to "combat stereotypes" and was supported by numerous large Hollywood corporations.[135]

Indeed, several Hollywood organizations did join forces with the AoC Media Fund. Some of the Fund's partners included Participant Productions: the company which produced the anti-American and pro-jihadist film "Syriana," International Creative Management: a Hollywood talent agency, Summit Entertainment: a Hollywood film distribution company, and YouTube.[136]

The Fund operated from January 2008 to October 2009. Subsequently, it merged with Solyia, a non-profit organization which continues its mission to foster "cross-cultural engagement," but now focuses on the use of innovative new media technologies rather than traditional Hollywood films in order to achieve its goals.[137] Nevertheless, the footprint created by the AoC Media Fund remains as it assisted with the start-up of the Unity Production's MOST initiative, which appears to be essentially an Islamic propaganda company (to be discussed in more detail later in this monograph).[138] MOST continues to operate to this day, long after the AoC's Media Fund has gone out of existence.

CHAPTER 6

UNITY PRODUCTIONS FOUNDATION

"Popular culture is a place where pity is called compassion, flattery is called love, propaganda is called knowledge, tension is called peace, gossip is called news, and auto-tune is called singing."

– Criss Jami

A New and Improved Islamic Supremacist Organization

Unity Productions Foundation is a non-profit film production company that insists that its mission is to "counter bigotry and promote peace through media."[139] Upon closer inspection, however, it appears that UPF is nothing more than an Islamic supremacist organization providing disinformation through faux "documentaries" to unwitting people in government, academia, faith communities and the general public.

UPF is a 501(c)(3) non-profit organization (meaning donations are tax-deductible), founded in 1999, which operates out of the Washington, DC area.[140] It was founded by Alex Kronemer, a former State Department employee and Michael Wolfe, a film producer, both of whom are Muslim converts. UPF is well funded to the tune of approximately three million dollars per year, out of which Kronemer and Wolfe draw their annual salaries of more than 200,000 dollars each.[141] UPF's funding comes largely from the Middle East and North Africa[142] as well as from U.S. government grants.[143]

UPF's films are part of UPF's long term so-called "educational campaigns"[144] to show Muslims in a more positive light. Its films are designed for TV, movie theaters and online viewings. It has shown thousands of film screenings in classrooms and civic institutions. To date, UPF has produced numerous full length films[145] presented as "documentaries" for the Public Broadcasting Network (PBS) as well as some shorter videos and one additional film made for theaters. The "documentaries" have been seen by approximately 150 million people, are of very high production quality, and have won dozens of awards nationally and internationally. These awards include but are not limited to Best Documentary at the 2007 American Black Film Festival, four Grand Goldies Awards, four CINE Golden Eagle Awards, Hamburg World Media Film Festival's Gold and Silver Awards, and the Newark Black Film Festival's 2008 Paul Robeson Award.[146]

Additionally, UPF works with Hollywood through its "Muslims on Screen and Television" (MOST) resource program (discussed in more detail later in the monograph) by providing its version of "facts" and "research" to scriptwriters and producers worldwide.[147]

UPF is also very active in the interfaith movement, partnering with prominent but naïve Jewish, Christian and Muslim interfaith organizations to run dialogues nationwide. The "20,000 Dialogues" program, spear-headed by UPF, boasts of over 80,000 participants in classrooms, community centers, religious congregations, government, and the general public.[148]

Though UPF touts itself as a production company, extensive research suggests its real mission is to provide pro-Islam propaganda and disinformation campaigns designed to influence all segments of society from government to faith communities. UPF's films are merely the mechanism by which this goal is achieved. These films are used in a myriad of initiatives to sway a variety of audiences targeted by UPF. Because UPF has significant funding and its founders are tightly connected to both the U.S. government and to Hollywood from their pre-UPF careers, UPF is quickly becoming a major player in the Islamic propaganda machine. It is increasingly successful at altering history and "facts" disseminated in the information battle-space, including on the internet, where in some cases, much of what is "known" is associated with UPF's faux documentaries.

UPF is one organization in particular that national security professionals, free speech advocates and general historians are advised to keep an eye on. TV stations, theaters, schools, churches and civic organizations that plan to show UPF's films should scrutinize the information set forth in these "documentaries" prior to holding screenings, rather than accept the narratives offered at face value.

UPF's Founders: The Dangerous Duo

Alex Kronemer is the Executive Producer and CEO for all UPF films. He is very active in UPF's "20,000 Dialogues" initiative, regularly making presentations at interfaith events. He is also well published in foreign media including that from Pakistan, Indonesia, and Egypt, as well as in liberal media outlets in America, such as the Huffington Post.[149] Formerly, he worked with the Bureau of Human Rights at the U.S. State Department and still has many connections there. Additionally, he was a founding member of the U.S. Institute of Peace.[150] In 1999-2000, Kronemer served as a U.S. Delegate to the UN Human Rights Commission and "was instrumental in briefing senior State Department and White House officials on issues related to Islam." It is Kronemer who was responsible for organizing the U.S. State Department's first Iftar dinner,[151] which was hosted by then-Secretary of State Madeline Albright.[152]

Michael Wolfe is the President of UPF and Co-Executive Producer for UPF Films as well as Director of UPF's MOST program.[153] He is a lecturer on the subject of Islam in universities including Harvard, Georgetown, Princeton and SUNY and has won numerous awards including one from MPAC.[154] He has also written several pro-Islam books.[155]

Other UPF staff members deliver multitudes of lectures, speeches, presentations and conferences at prestigious universities such at Georgetown University, American University, Stanford University, Princeton University and Duke University.[156] Many of them also write articles on Islam-related subjects[157] undoubtedly with a pro-Islam bent.

UPF's Programs

The following provides a brief description of various UPF programs and their ties to different sectors of society. These initiatives demonstrate the true purpose of UPF's film production, to be used as a vehicle to manipulate its target audiences to view Islam in a positive light and inoculate all spheres of society against Islam's violent, intolerant and anti-freedom aspects.

Outreach to Teachers

For each film produced by UPF, the organization also creates "lesson plans," interactive websites and other "teaching" resources for teachers at the high school and college levels. Probably not coincidently, funding is provided largely by Kronemer's prior employer, the U.S. Institute for Peace, as well as by the National Endowment for the Humanities.[158]

20,000 Dialogues

UPF has numerous outreach programs purportedly designed to "educate" policy-makers, academia and the general public. These programs use UPF films to prompt "dialogue" among audience members. UPF has several initiatives which it refers to collectively as "20,000 Dialogues." [159] UPF's "20,000 Dialogues" partners with over 300 universities, student groups, interfaith groups, academic and community leaders as well as artists and professionals.[160]

Because the films shown are replete with falsehoods and misleading information (to be discussed later in the monograph), it is reasonable to conclude that the programs themselves accordingly consist of disinformation, indoctrination, and false narratives targeting every level of society.

Briefly, the initiatives are as follows:

1) "Training Programs Tailored for Organizations" is a program of utmost significance for both those who support or oppose UPF's agenda. It lays out the basics by reviewing UPF's definitions of "terminology" and "key facts" about American Muslims and Islam, and goes on to produce strategies for "community building" and "understanding."

It's important to understand that language is the frontline battlefield in the war of ideas because how words are defined will determine whether or not the underlying concepts are properly understood. To illustrate, in matters of national security, properly naming the enemy is a critical pre-requisite, necessary to produce a sound strategy of defeat.

It is no coincidence that many Islamic supremacist organizations, such as the Organization of Islamic Cooperation, Muslim

Brotherhood front-groups and UPF are working fastidiously to redefine, control, and silence speech through the manipulation of lexicon and the mischaracterization of words.[161] One of the goals of these groups is to dissociate the word "Islam" from the word "terrorism," denying the existence of Islamic terrorism [162] in an apparent attempt to disarm America's national security apparatus.

Additionally, when an organization purports to support free speech, the organization must be compelled to define its terms and be clear about what types of speech it considers protected versus unprotected speech. [163] Though many Islamic supremacist organizations claim to support freedom of speech, in the next breath they insist that free speech does not include "offensive speech," "hate speech," "Islamophobic speech" or Islamic blasphemy. They therefore make a mockery of America's First Amendment.

Further, as with all propaganda outfits, sprinkled amidst UPF's factual propositions, are questionable or erroneous "facts" as well, otherwise known as "disinformation." Therefore, a program like this is potentially dangerous as it can provide inaccurate information to policy professionals in the think tank world that UPF is purporting to "educate."

2) "My Fellow American" is an initiative to combat so-called "Islamophobia" using a UPF video. Participants in the film include Evangelical and Catholic leaders who are concerned about "Islamophobia,"[164] which is usually ill-defined or not defined at all. Therefore, the entire concept behind this project is inherently flawed.

Westerners often assume that "Islamophobia" means "bigotry against Muslims." But when tracked, it is clear that the Islamic organizations making accusations of "Islamophobia" are clearly applying the word in a manner that is synonymous with Islamic blasphemy. Anything that sheds Islam in a negative light, even if true, is smeared with the label "Islamophobic" by the OIC,[165] Muslim Brotherhood front groups and other Islamic apologists. The character of those with legitimate concerns about Islamic terrorism, Islamic persecution of religious minorities or human rights violations committed in the name of Islam, are often impugned with name-calling and false accusations.

3) "Understanding Muslim Diversity" is a program that uses the factually and analytically flawed UPF films[166] to "train" those at the highest levels of government in the "cultural competency of Muslim Americans." This program specifically targets law enforcement, national security professionals, intelligence professionals and policy makers. Unfortunately, the National Counterterrorism Center, the Pentagon, the United Nations, and the Boston Police Department, and additional agencies have all bought into the politically correct belief that they should indoctrinate their staff with multiculturalism. Accordingly, UPF has made presentations to each of these agencies.[167]

4) "Ground Zero Dialogue" is an initiative which commenced in response to opposition against building the Ground Zero Mosque on the ash-heaps of the fallen World Trade Center towers, which collapsed as a result of the largest Islamic terrorist attack on American soil on September 11, 2011. The initiative is a social media campaign created to push pro-Islam sentiment and provide Muslims with resources to help disseminate their viewpoints.[168]

5) "Prince Among Slaves: the Cultural Legacy of Enslaved African Americans" is a website with various themes to promote "dialogue" on relevant Islam-related issues, and which utilizes a UPF produced film that goes by the same name. [169] The film holding this title presents a skewed narrative that will be discussed in more depth later in this chapter.

Muslims on Screen and Television[170]

UPF works with Hollywood through its separately incorporated organization based in Hollywood, called "MOST," an acronym for "Muslims on Screen and Television." MOST is a "resource center" for movie and television producers and screen-writers, providing free "research, information and expert consultations ... on any of their characters or storylines regarding Muslims, Islam or the Middle East." [171]

MOST's stated goal is to combat "stereotypes" of Muslims in the media and control how Muslims are portrayed. Toward this end, it provides a "storybank" of pre-selected stories that portray Muslims in a positive light. The Hollywood community can locate these at the touch of a mouse, free of charge. MOST also provides phone consultations which disseminate one-sided "facts, polls, and research," that support its point of view.[172]

Additionally, MOST holds events on Islam-related issues while providing an opportunity for policy-makers and Hollywood agents, actors, screen-writers and producers to mingle. The aim is to "engage" both the Hollywood community and policy leaders in "dialogue" regarding Islam and Muslims.[173]

MOST was founded in 2007 by the Saban Center for Middle East Policy at the Brookings Institute, UPF, the Alliance of Civilizations Media Fund, the Gallup Muslims West Project, and the Russell Family Foundation. [174] All of the organizations that have partnered with MOST are of like mind, and have in common that part of their mission is to provide a pre-determined notion of Islam and Muslims in the West, rather than following the facts where ever they might lead.[175]

MOST never shows Muslims or Islam as anything other than categorically positive. Clearly, its goal is not to include myriad viewpoints or to provide objective information. Rather, MOST attempts to change the way Islam and Muslims are portrayed in the media, making these more positive (even if biased), and to control the narrative—whether its supporting "facts" are accurate or not.

UPF Partners with Muslim Brotherhood Front Groups

UPF works with a variety of organizations across the board from those in the interfaith movement, law enforcement, federal agencies, as well as Muslim Brotherhood front groups that believe Islam is superior to other religions and that Muslims should have preferential treatment. UPF's film premiere events are often co-hosted or co-sponsored by Islamic supremacist groups including the International Institute of Islamic Thought, The Muslim Students Association, and the Islamic Society of North America,[176] all of which are Muslim Brotherhood-affiliated groups cited in the 1991 Explanatory Memorandum.[177]

UPF has additional connections to these groups as well. In the past, UPF CEO Alex Kronemer was a speaker at an ISNA Annual Convention,[178] as was UPF staff member Daniel Tutt.[179] In 2016, UPF sponsored a booth at the ISNA Convention's Bazaar.[180] That ISNA was named by the Justice Department as an unindicted co-conspirator in the 2008 Holy Land Foundation trial,[181] the largest terror financing trial in the history of the United States, has not dissuaded UPF from working with this organization. Joined by the likes of UPF and enabled by U.S. government agencies, ISNA continues to operate with impunity.

UPF also has also joined forces in partnership with the Bridge Initiative,[182] an "anti-Islamophobia" program housed within Georgetown University's Prince Alwaleed Center for Muslim-Christian Understanding.[183] Saudi Arabia's Prince Alwaleed bin Talal donated approximately 20 million dollars to the Center, which helps line the pockets of Islamic apologist John Esposito, the Center's Founding Director [184] and the current Project Director for the Center's Bridge Initiative.[185] The funds come from the same Prince Alwaleed whose offer of 10 million dollars to NYC after 9/11 was turned down by Mayor Giuliani because Alwaleed blamed the terrorist attack on U.S. foreign policy.[186] The Kingdom of Saudi Arabia also arrested and detained the Prince, along with several others, in early November, 2017, as part of a sweeping anti-corruption initiative.[187]

Analysis:
UPF's "Documentaries":
A Mixture of Truth and Fiction

UPF's "documentaries" are replete with errors and half-truths. Americans are generally naïve. Many assume that films presented as documentaries are necessarily accurate and true. Though they haven't heard the stories before, few will set out to research and double check the facts presented. Yet, it does not take much research to discover that the films make false assertions and fabrications that support the narratives they seek to impose on an unsuspecting public.

UPF and MOST have been successful in attracting large funders to contribute to the production of their films, and to entice high level government officials to appear at their opening nights, often on panels for their high profile events. The producers' connections to the State Department, U.S. government agencies, Hollywood, and PBS, have also yielded high profile participation in UPF programs and events as well as endorsements of UPF films. That some of the film programs have been co-sponsored by Muslim Brotherhood front-groups or groups that seek the spread of shariah, has not dissuaded government officials or Hollywood elites from participation.[188]

A few examples of UPF's faux documentaries follow. Please note that each documentary contains a combination of accurate information and false or misleading information, thus following the recipe for what those in national security refer to as "disinformation."

UPF Film:
Noor Inayat Khan: Enemy of the Reich

Washington, D.C. Premiere

UPF and MOST often have celebrated "premiere" events to open their films in big cities around the country. The world premiere for *Noor Inayat Khan: Enemy of the Reich* was shown at the prestigious Warner Theatre on February 15, 2014.[189] Speakers included (but were not limited to) Rashad Hussein, U.S. envoy to the Organization of Islamic Cooperation, Ira Forman, Special envoy to Monitor and Combat anti-Semitism, [190] and a surprise visit by Eileen O'Connor, Assistant Secretary of State for South and Central Asia (not listed on the program). The themes expressed by the various speakers lumped antisemitism and "Islamophobia" together (wrongly assuming their root causes were analogous), talked about the need to increase "interfaith dialogue," and asserted the notion that Noor Khan was motivated by her "Muslim faith" to "save Jews" during the Holocaust.[191] And, though there is no doubt that Noor Khan was indeed a hero, research reveals that this "documentary" was replete with half-truths and falsehoods, especially regarding Khan's "faith."

Narrated by Academy Award winning actress Helen Mirren, and produced by three time Emmy Award winner Robert H. Gardner, *Enemy of the Reich* tells the story of a woman with courage, love of humanity, and the highest morals and ideals.[192]

Noor Khan's Background

Noor Khan was born in Russia and spent her early years in England and then France. When the Nazis invaded France, in 1940, the Khan family fled back to the United Kingdom. Noor joined the Women's Auxiliary Air Force (WAAF) and became a wireless operator. Three years later, she was recruited to the Special Operations Executive (SOE) in France, and worked under an assumed name.

The job was a dangerous, but served a critical function in service to the Allied cause against the Nazis. She, like other wireless operators, was in constant danger of being captured and killed. Khan accepted her mission, despite knowing its risks. After all the other operators in her unit were captured by the Nazi intelligence agency (SD), Khan refused an offer to return to Britain. She remained in France as the sole French wireless operator and the only radio operator linking the British to the French Resistance. The Nazis went after her in hot pursuit.[193] She could only transmit for twenty minutes at a time, before having to move to another station to evade capture.[194]

After four months on the job, she was betrayed by a French collaborator who turned her in to the SD. In September, 1943 she was arrested by the Gestapo and interrogated for over a month, but she refused to provide the SS with any information.[195] She twice escaped and was recaptured. She was then sent to a Nazi prison camp in Germany.[196] There, she was shackled and condemned to solitary confinement for ten months, but still she refused to cooperate with the SS.[197]

In September of 1944, Khan was transported to the Dachau concentration camp, where she was murdered by gun shot two days later. Her last recorded word was "[L]iberté!"[198]

Khan was 30 years old when the Nazis killed her. She became one of the SOE's most decorated agents and was undoubtedly a hero. She was given many posthumous awards including the British George Cross, the French Croix de Guerre. She was commemorated on a British stamp themed "remarkable lives" and a bust of Khan was erected in London's Garden Square.[199]

Khan's Motivation

According to UPF's co-founder, CEO and Executive Producer, Alex Kronemer, Khan's courage, integrity, and zeal in her quest against Nazism was motivated by her "Muslim faith." Though *Enemy of the Reich* does not expressly make this assertion, the film, which consists primarily of interviews, is replete with this insinuation. Additionally, a brochure obtained from UPF proclaims that Khan's story is "rooted in Islam."[200]

In his opening statements at the film's Washington DC premiere, Kronemer asked why Khan would risk her life and what would compel her to put herself in potential danger to "save the Jews." His answer was her faith. "What compelled her was her great sense of humanity for other people, religions, other races, and Nazi ideology was opposed to her beliefs." Kronemer claimed that in recent years, stories of Muslims hiding Jews to save them during the Holocaust had come to his attention. He wondered why he had never heard of any stories about the role of Muslims in World War II. He argued that he produced this film, as well as other pro-Muslim and pro-Islam films to "tell the full story" of Muslims.[201] *Enemy of the Reich* is the tenth such film.[202]

Many interviewed in the film asserted that Khan's motivation was "idealism" or "her ideology." She believed that all life has value and she had a tolerant view of all religions. Her nephew, who is Sufi, assumed "it must have been her faith. Only that faith could have carried her… Her message is that the human soul is of Divine Source, all humans must be free, and every human is sacrosanct." Indeed, prior to becoming a British spy, Khan built a career writing children's stories, which taught that all conflict should be resolved through love and non-violence.[203]

Unfortunately, there are numerous flaws with the film's assertions. While it is true that Khan appeared to be motivated by her belief system as many people are, it is inaccurate to assume that only people of "faith" have virtue and courage. And, research reveals that Khan was not a devout Muslim. In fact, she was not a practicing Muslim at all.[204]

Khan grew up in a home with an Indian Sufi father and an American mother. Her father's brand of Islam was a far cry from traditional or authoritative Islam and indeed, it would be considered heretical by traditional Islamic standards,[205] perhaps even warranting imprisonment or execution.

Contrary to the film's proclamation that "Sufis are first and foremost Muslim," Khan's father's version of Sufism expressly disavows belonging to any particular religion including Islam. He belonged to the Christi Order within the mystic tradition, which emphasizes love, tolerance and openness. It is known for welcoming seekers of all faiths, and confines itself to no particular doctrine or ideology, including Islam. It emphasizes the universality of all faith traditions, not favoring one over another. It seeks to spread the message of unity and the divinity in all living beings. Her father believed that there is really only one universal religion and there are many paths to God. He was primarily concerned with the inner soul, not shariah. So even if Khan were "religious" in the same sense that her father was, it would be inaccurate to conclude that her faith was "Islamic" in any true meaning of the word.[206]

The producer of the film could only conclude that Khan was Muslim by the assuming that all Sufis are Muslim and then extrapolating that Khan's father was Sufi and thus Muslim, so Khan must have been also. According to Sharabani Basu, author of Khan's biography titled "Spy Princess: the life of Noor Inayat Khan," however, Khan was not a "practicing Muslim" of any stripe, despite the fact that she was influenced by her liberal Sufi upbringing.[207]

Additionally, the film conspicuously omits the fact that Khan was engaged to a Jew prior to the outbreak of World War II. It's hard to believe that this was an accidental oversight on the part of UPF, rather than the intentional omission of information that would tip off the audience to the fact that Khan could not have been the devout Muslim that UPF claims she was. Islamic doctrine dictates that while Muslim men are permitted to marry Jewish or Christian women, Muslim women are confined to marry Muslim men only.[208]

That Khan's marriage to her fiancé never came to fruition is of no consequence. What is important is the fact that Khan, while certainly motivated by a loving, virtuous ideology, was not motivated by Islam as UPF producers would have the audience think. *Enemy of the Reich* holds itself out

44

as honoring this courageous Holocaust heroine. But on some level, it stains her memory by attributing to her false motives, in a narrative that constitutes nothing more than Islamic propaganda.[209]

UPF Film:
Muhammad: The Legacy of a Prophet

Produced in 2002 by UPF, this film asserts that Muhammad was the "most generous-hearted of men, the most truthful of them in speech, the most mild tempered of them, the noblest of them in lineage."[210]

The film claims to tell the history of the Muslim Prophet Muhammad and his relevance today, as told through the eyes of those interviewed.[211] Virtually all of the interviewees consisted of apologists for Islamic supremacism or those who were sympathetic to its cause.

The narratives were rife with misleading, erroneous or incomplete "facts." For example, Karen Armstrong, leftist historian and known apologist for Islam, stated that during Muhammad's time there "was violence and killing"[212] without explaining who and what caused it. Of course, most of the violence and killing to which she referred was initiated by the Muslim Prophet Muhammad and his followers in Medina. Following Muhammad's lead as a soldier and warrior, rather than simply a spiritual leader, his followers comprised an army. Armstrong went on to say that Muhammad "single-handedly ... brought peace and a new hope to Arabia" and served as "a new beacon to the world."[213] The truth is that Islam conquered Arabia primarily by the sword, not through persuasion. [214] Any "peace" that was had, was brought about by chasing non-Muslims out of the land, coercing them to convert to Islam, or bringing them under the dual-system of law known as "dhimmitude" whereby Jews and Christians live in second class citizenry in exchange for temporary peace.[215]

The film talks about the effect Muhammad's life has on the "estimated 7 million Muslims in America." This number is wildly inflated, however, especially for when cited in 2002. As of 2016, the PEW research Center, hardly a right-wing outfit, estimates that the current number of Muslims in America hovers around 3.3 million, approximately 1 percent of the U.S. population.[216]

Michael Wolfe, co-producer of the film, stated that Muhammad is the "source of how to behave, how to be a constructive citizen, how to be a good parent." Jameel Johnson, Chief of Staff to then-Democrat Congressman

Gregory Meeks, explained that Muhammad demonstrates the exemplary standard of behavior and the Qur'an is the "guide to how we deal with each other, and *when we're in a position of authority,* how we attempt to implement *justice and law.*"[217] What the film doesn't explain is that, according to Muslim Brotherhood documents as well as Muhammad's example (as related in the *Sunna*), when Muslims are in a position of authority – in other words, when they are in the majority – their implementation of "justice and law" means the implementation of shariah. Indeed, the Muslim Brotherhood's political party is called the Party for Freedom and Justice.[218] Yet its version of "justice," "law" and "freedom" and America's concept of justice, law and freedom could not be farther apart.[219]

Other interviewees included Daisy Khan who, together with her husband Faisal Abdul Rauf jointly spearheaded the effort to place a mosque at the site of Ground Zero; John Voll, an Islamic apologist who teaches at Georgetown University (home to the Prince Alwaleed bin Talal Center for Muslim – Christian Understanding); and Imam Al-Qazwini who, in 2015, resigned from his post at the Islamic Center of America because its board refused to liberalize. As he explained, "We talk about Islam being progressive, but … in the heart of America, in the largest Islamic Center of America, women have no role at all."[220]

The film also show-cased Anwar Al-Awlaki, a former American imam who preached fiery sermons at the Dar al-Hijrah mosque in Virginia. Considered a spiritual advisor to several 9/11 hijackers as well as to Nidal Hasan, (the Fort Hood jihadist), Al-Awlaki had close ties to Muslim Brotherhood front-groups. He joined Al-Qaeda and was eventually killed in Yemen by the Obama Administration in a targeted assassination.[221]

The Legacy of a Prophet was funded by PBS and a host of questionable characters including the Sabadia Family Foundation, the El-Hibri Foundation and the Qureishi Family Trust.[222] The El-Hibris work in the defense industry and have access to non-nuclear weapons of mass destruction, own a company called "Emergent Bio-Solutions," and supported the Obama campaign. Fuad El-Hibri donated to Obama's campaign, and his aunt Azizah El-Hibri was appointed by President Obama to the Commission on International Religious freedom as a Commissioner, despite her Islamic supremacist views.[223]

Azizah El-Hibri also heads up "Karamah," which characterizes itself as a "feminist" organization concerning itself with the rights of Muslim women.[224] In recent years, Karamah screened a film which pushed for the "education" of Muslim girls in the Middle East. The film advocated the idea that little girls should have the opportunity to learn and memorize the Qur'an just as boys do, in the name of "equal rights." When the interviewer in the film asked one of the little girls what Allah thought of Jews, however, she stated that he thinks they are apes and pigs, as stated in the Qur'an. This didn't seem to bother anybody in Karamah's discussion group, which consisted primarily of hijabbed women.[225]

Additionally, Azizah El-Hibri has been a speaker at interfaith dialogue groups, giving the impression that America is bigoted against Muslims.[226] Previously, she served on the board of the American Muslim Council, a Muslim Brotherhood front-group headed by Abdulrahman Alamoudi who now sits in jail on terrorism related charges.[227] It should be no surprise that Karamah is a recipient of funding by Prince Alwaleed bin Talal of Saudi Arabia,[228] who, in the past, has donated millions of dollars to the pro-Islam biased Center for Muslim-Christian Understanding at Georgetown University, and asserted that 9/11 was the fault of America's foreign policy.

Additionally, Azizah El-Hibri has expressed support for Sayyid Qutb, founder of the Muslim Brotherhood, and has actively fought against U.S. counterterrorism measures.[229] The El-Hibri Family Foundation has taken the money it made on defense contracts (via taxpayer dollars) and funneled it into propaganda films produced by UPF.[230]

The Sabadia family is also involved in the defense industry. Sabtech Industries, owned by Pakistani born Rahim Sabadia, lost its security clearance after making questionable donations to so-called Muslim "charities," which often funnel money to terrorist organizations. Additionally, the Sabadia Family Foundation is a huge donor to the Hamas-linked CAIR.[231]

Safi Quereshy, a Pakistani born computer company entrepreneur,[232] has also been actively involved with CAIR and ISNA,[233] both named unindicted co-conspirators in the Holy Land Foundation terror financing trial by the Justice Department.

Muhammad: The Legacy of the Prophet touts Muhammad in his role as merchant, husband and warrior.[234] It fails to mention the wonton murder, polygamy, child-marriage and plunder that he is documented as having committed in these roles.

This film was first aired on PBS in 2002 and has since been re-aired to over 600 PBS and individual stations around the country. It has been used in presentations to thousands of schools, colleges, "civic organizations" and religious congregations "to increase Americans' understanding of Muslims and Islam."[235] It also has a guide to assist discussion groups which is provided by

UPF's 20,000 Dialogues Project and The Islam Project. In 2011, a DVD of the film was re-released and now includes "lesson plans" for the classroom.[236]

The blatant omissions in the reporting content of this film demonstrate the clear bias of those who created it. It is said that half a truth constitutes a whole lie. This film cherry picks what it reports about the Muslim Prophet Muhammad and leaves out his blueprint for the terrorism, human rights violations and discrimination that is emulated by the Global Jihad Movement today. Despite this, the film has worked its way into schools created to educate the youth of America. The disinformation disseminated through these films will create the narratives that leaders of tomorrow will take with them into the future. It is nothing less than dangerous.

UPF Film:
Prince Among Slaves

Prince Among Slaves was co-produced in 2006 by UPF, Spark Media[237] (a left-wing social advocacy film production company) and Duke Media[238] (an organization focusing on teaching African American youth the ins and outs of the film industry). It was largely funded by a grant from the National Endowment of Humanities won the "Best Documentary" Award at the American Black Film Festival in Los Angeles, 2007. It also was aired on PBS to kick off Black History Month in 2008. [239]

This film is yet another propaganda film set forth by UPF. It tells the story of a "Muslim Prince," Abdul Rahman Ibrahima Sori, who after being captured in West Africa, fell from his life of privilege and esteemed position in the military, to suffer 40 years of enslavement in Mississippi. Though eventually he won his freedom, he was only partially successful in his attempts to secure freedom for his extended family, with some freed and some not. Eventually, the "Prince" returned to Africa, where he continued to fight for his family's release. [240]

The film targets an African-American audience and characterizes the Prince's history as an example of Negro slave heritage, in an attempt to convince African-Americans that their cultural background is Muslim. [241] Toward this end, the film holds up Prince Rahman as a role model of bravery and courage.[242] Unfortunately, the film, while peppered with some truths, is simply another example of distorted facts pumped out by UPF, twisted around to hold out the desired narrative as reality.

Though Rahman was indeed a slave, he was hardly a role model for the African-American community. He considered himself neither Negro nor Muslim. Despite his dark coloring, he looked down on Negroes, insisting that not a drop of Negro blood ran through his veins. Instead, he considered himself a Moor, and made it clear that he viewed Negroes on a scale significantly beneath Moors. [243]

Even worse, prior to his capture, Rahman was a mass murderer of Negro Africans, razed their towns, and had a blood thirsty disposition. [244] Eventually, when he lost a battle with the Africans he was attacking, they caught him and sold him into slavery. [245] At some point during his captivity, Rahman was made manager of the plantation where he worked because of his education. Nevertheless, Mr. Foster, the plantation owner, had to keep an eye on Rahman due to his propensity for cruelty against the slaves over whom he had power.[246]

Though he was able to write a little bit in Arabic and appears to have been born of Muslim descent, Rahman spoke very highly of Christianity, promising to help spread it in America. [247]

While the film condemns the enslavement of African Muslims, it's important to note that many Muslims, including African Muslims were also slave owners. Indeed, it was Arab Muslims who enslaved blacks hundreds of years before Europe did, forced them to convert to Islam under threat of torture, and later sold them to North Americans.[248]

It was Christianity, and not Islam, that eventually led the abolition movement to free all slaves. [249] In Islam, it is permissible to take non-Muslims, including children, as the spoils of war when violent jihad is won.[250] In fact, the Muslim Prophet Muhammad had dozens of slaves.[251] Though later Caliphs condemned the practice of enslaving Muslims, the Islamic practice of enslaving non-Muslims continues in some countries to this day.[252] It is still openly practiced in the Islamic Republics of Mauritania and Sudan, [253] and though illegal, there is evidence of its continued practice in Saudi Arabia, Yemen, Oman, Niger[254] and the UAE.[255] It is therefore ironic that the film "Prince of Slaves" tries to laud Islam as the heritage of black Africans, when many of those who do have a Muslim heritage, have it due to conversion under coercion and abuse, rather than choice.

Today, what little was known about Prince Rahman is getting lost amidst UPF's propaganda which has flooded the Internet. A quick Google search will demonstrate that much of the "information" on the Prince is associated with UPF's film. It obfuscates the truth about Muslim slavery of Negroes and exalts this cruel, racist slave-holder, transforming him into an idol for African-Americans to emulate. This could only have been achieved by pushing false narratives and omitting crucial facts.

In addition to being a film, *Prince Among Slaves* also constitutes a website by the same name. This website is used by UPF's 20,000 Dialogues program to foster discussion on the falsehoods it perpetuates. [256]

Connecting Cultures, LLC

Alex Kronemer's wife, Lobna "Luby" Ismail, is the founder of Connecting Cultures, LLC. With a Masters in "Intercultural Relations" from Lesley College in Massachusetts, she markets herself as a training specialist in "Islamic awareness and religious diversity," "Arab and American cultures" and "cross cultural communication."[257]

Her staff consists of her, her husband (UPF's President, Alex Kronemer), and Mr. Jean Abinader, an expert in "strategic communication" with experience in training government agencies at home and abroad. He is an advisor to many U.S. government agencies, focusing on issues related to Arab and Muslim countries. [258]

Luby was critical to the development of UPF's 20,000 Dialogues program and its Ground Zero Dialogue program, both of which support her work. Luby prides herself on having trained "hundreds of law enforcement and military officers on both Arab and Muslim Americans."[259] Indeed, as a Government Services Administration-approved contractor, [260] CC's website boasts of training U.S. government agencies including the State Department, the Department of Homeland Security, the Army, the FBI, the U.S. Marines, the Transportation Security Agency, and the Department of Justice (DOJ) among others.[261]

During the Obama years, CC "trained" the Department of Justice and hundreds of U.S. Attorneys across the country on alleged "misperceptions" about Islam and Muslims.[262] CC's programs and workshops emphasize issues such as how not to cause Muslims offense, how to ensure that product designs of Islamic imagery is "respectful" and not insulting, and how to respond to Muslim religious accommodation requests such as prayer times.[263] Under the guise of "respect," the program appears to be advocating censorship and cloaked in the language of "religious freedom" or "religious accommodation," the program urges what many consider preferential treatment for Muslims.

CC's law enforcement video tries to normalize "cultural differences" so that police officers, in effect, give a pass to Muslims who behave in a way that would be unacceptable if exhibited by non-Muslims. [264] All of this might explain why former U.S. Attorney General Eric Holder was unable to answer a simple question when testifying at a Congressional hearing, as to whether "radical Islam" might be one of the causes of terrorism. [265] Perusing CC's website of training programs and test questions, it's not hard to see that these consist of one-sided indoctrination seminars, getting through under the politically correct multiculturalism umbrella designed to provide Muslims with special privileges which are not extended to Americans of other faiths.

In conclusion, UPF's staff is heavily connected to and engaged in the indoctrination of all sectors of society, not the least of which is law enforcement. Many of the "progressive" key staff-members at government agencies, production companies, law enforcement agencies, and academic "training" programs share the same goal of providing politically correct disinformation regarding Islam that results in it attaining an exalted status.

UPF: Conclusion

The more that is uncovered about UPF, the clearer it becomes that UPF is much more than a production company. Research suggests it is a full-fledged influence operation. The films it produces appear to be simply the vehicles through which to conduct its disinformation campaigns.

UPF is not like other Muslim Brotherhood organizations which are used to being publicly lambasted from conservative national security quarters. UPF is not an unindicted co-conspirator like CAIR or ISNA, and with the exception of a few isolated articles, its deceptive practices have been largely overlooked and unreported. Therefore, UPF is unaccustomed to being criticized in the media or the public sphere.

To the contrary, UPF often receives accolades for its work. It is very connected to Hollywood, PBS, the State Department, the Department of Justice and law enforcement. It is well-funded and intertwined with various left-wing movements including the "interfaith," "engagement," and "dialogue" movements. It enjoys an air of legitimacy that it does not deserve. These are all signs of a successful influence operation that must be countered. Exposure of the lies and propaganda is the first step to undermining UPF's influence. This monograph undertakes that task.

CHAPTER 7

ISLAMIC SCHOLARSHIP FUND

ISF: Penetrating the Film Industry

The Islamic Scholarship Fund (ISF) is another organization that is working hard to change the public perception of Islam and Muslims by injecting itself into the movie-making industry, in addition to other means.[266]

By its own admission, ISF's mission is to recruit more Muslims into the fields of journalism, politics, film production and academia to "properly represent Islam and Muslims in the U.S." ISF openly states that its goal is to "increase the number of Muslims obtaining jobs in the public policy and public opinion shaping professions."[267]

ISF is a non-profit organization whose stated mission is to "address the underrepresentation of American Muslims in the fields and occupations that influence public opinion and make public policy." [268] Considering that Muslims constitute a mere one percent of the population,[269] however, it hardly seems that Muslims in these fields are truly "underrepresented." Yet, the organization's mission statement could not constitute a better or more forthright way to convey that the organization was created for the overt purpose of conducting influence operations.[270]

ISF's Programs of Influence

Toward this end, ISF has several programs. One of them is its Film Grants program, which expressly references the mass media's "undoubtedly powerful influence on society's perception and beliefs." Accordingly, the ISF Film Grant is intended to fund Muslim film-makers who desire to create films which tell positive stories about Muslims. Those who work on "documentaries" are awarded a grant of 10,000 dollars; those who work on "narratives" are awarded a grant of 20,000 dollars. One of the prerequisites to receive a grant is that the subject matter of the film portrays "a unique vision creating a positive light for Muslims."[271]

To understand exactly what ISF is, it's important to be familiar with some of its associations and activities which are unrelated to the film industry. ISF partners with the Muslim Brotherhood front-group MPAC to offer a "congressional leadership development program" (CLDP). This program places Muslims in congressional internship positions for the purpose of gaining an "insider's" view about how to effectuate social change. The program provides networking opportunities, mentorship, and a speaker series to give Muslim political aspirants a leg up in achieving their political professional goals, hoping to "cultivate" the next generation of congressmen, mayors and other positions of power.[272]

Additionally, ISF offers a Scholarship program for students who are "active in the Muslim community," by which ISF means that the scholarships are exclusively available to those who are members of specifically listed Islamic centers.[273] It should be noted that most "Islamic Centers" have Muslim Brotherhood affiliated ties, and function at least in part, as Da'wa organizations. As stated in the 1991 Explanatory Memorandum, written by a Muslim Brotherhood member: the Islamic Center is the "axis" of the Islamic Movement and its role is to become a "House of Da'wa."[274]

The scholarships do not apply to all fields but are limited to those who want to pursue Islamic advocacy, and are majoring in an ISF-approved major toward this end.[275] Therefore, the approved ISF majors are those where Islamic influence can be most felt: law, film-making, public policy, international relations, law and the like.[276]

Partnering with Muslim Brotherhood Fronts

In addition to offering joint scholarships with Islamic Centers and mosques, ISF lists several Muslim Brotherhood front-groups and other Islamic supremacist organizations as resources. They include but are not limited to ISNA,[277] CAIR, MPAC, and UPF,[278] the listings of which can be reasonably interpreted as tacit endorsement of these organizations.

Further revealing its supremacist agenda is ISF's board of directors. It includes among others, Michael Wolfe, co-founder of UPF, and Dr. Hatem Bazian, who teaches at the University of California in Berkeley[279] and is a rabid anti-Israel advocate. At one point Dr. Bazian was also head of Berkeley's Muslim Students Association[280] the very first Muslim Brotherhood front group founded in the U.S.[281]

54

By encouraging activists in the Islamic Ummah to conduct or participate in successful influence operations and rewarding them with money in the form of scholarships and grants, ISF is a perfect role model for Islamic supremacist organizations that seek to infiltrate the filmmaking, academic and political professions.

CHAPTER 8

THE HOLLYWOOD-ISLAMIST ALLIANCE

Hollywood Initiative to Combat Stereotypes of Muslims?

In July of 2008, the Iran Times reported that there was a "move underway in Hollywood to attack American stereotypes of Muslims and the effort is not being mounted by Muslims." According to the article, the effort was being "launched" by the Writers Guild in Hollywood along with the Brookings Institute (via its Saban Center for Middle East Policy). The article noted that the Center was started by Chaim Saban, who is a television producer, a "political fundraiser" and a Jew.[282]

Ostensibly, the launch event constituted a discussion panel of "writers, producers and filmmakers" formed to determine ways that Hollywood could break the "stereotype cycle."

Howard Gordon, Executive Producer of the award-winning Fox TV series "24," stated he was a recent convert on the issue.[283] Supposedly he "changed his mind" after (sue-happy) CAIR met with him and argued that portraying Muslims as terrorists would cause "anti-Muslim" prejudice.[284] "Fear sells," Gordon explained.

Post-CAIR, he now speaks out against "anti-Muslim stereotyping" in the media. He has even gone as far as joining forces with Participant Media to persuade other writers and producers to stop perpetuating these so-called "stereotypes.[285] Participant Media[286] and Howard Gordon also teamed up to produce Syriana, [287] the pro-terrorist Hollywood film, starring George Clooney.

Gordon explained that increasingly, Arab-American actors are turning down roles as Muslim terrorists. Eventually, Gordon began incorporating the ideas that his Arab and Muslim actors provided to him.[288] Additionally, the Iran Times article claimed that some "analysts" believe that American movie-goers are flooded with "relentless labeling and negative images" of Muslims. [289]

Purportedly, the purpose of the panel was to promote a series of "dialogues" where "experts" could explain Islam to those in the Hollywood entertainment industry. Yet, several participants in the program argued that the problem emanating from the Middle East should not be identified as Islam, but as a broader "East-West Divide." Thus, the panel was titled: "Rewriting the Divide."[290]

What Really Happened
(Who Was Behind the Initiative)

In fact, though the Writers Guild hosted this panel, contrary to the article's claim, the "effort" to combat "Muslim stereotypes" in Hollywood was indeed launched by Muslims. The panel event featured a film produced by UPF's MOST during one of its premieres.

The description of panelists as Hollywood "writers, producers and directors" was misleading. The panel consisted of: Michael Wolf, UPF Producer (Muslim), Dalia Mogahed of the Gallup Center for Muslim Studies,[291] Jim Berk from Participant Media, and Howard Gordon.[292]

Gordon, who had previously been pressured by CAIR to censor scenes from his hit TV series "24," admitted that part of his "conversion" was a business decision stemming from the fact that Muslim and Arab actors were refusing the roles he was writing.[293]

The event was clearly part of UPF's MOST program, [294] which, as previously discussed, appears to be an influence operations program aimed at Hollywood.[295] The article's characterization of the event and those behind it was clearly, but not surprisingly, false, and that false narrative was then repeated by the likes of CAIR.

Muslim Actors in Hollywood

Increasingly, actors of Arab descent are rejecting roles that cast them as Islamic terrorists. Some claim that agents have told them that unless they change their names, the only work that Muslims or Arabs will find in Hollywood is playing the role of Islamic terrorists.[296] Of course, it would be difficult to know whether or not these conversations really took place. But, it's misleading to argue that the phenomenon of actors Americanizing their names for purposes of box office appeal has been confined to Muslims and Middle Easterners.[297]

Articles giving voice to complaints made by Muslims and Arabs about the scant roles available to them ignore the fact that there are relatively few

58

Muslims and Arabs in the acting profession[298] and that the odds of "making it" in Hollywood are against everyone, no matter what their religion or ethnicity.

Still, despite refusals to Americanize their names, Muslim actors like Ahmed-Ahmed, an Egyptian-American actor based in Los Angeles, wound up being fairly successful. Ahmed-Ahmed was cast in in the block-buster film "Iron Man" with Robert Downey Jr.[299] and had a role in "You Don't Mess Around with Zohan" which starred Adam Sandler.[300] Other Muslim actors destined to Hollywood success who clearly have been unimpeded by anti-Muslim bigotry include Dave Shapell, Janet Jackson, Shoreh Aghdashloo[301] and Omar Sharif.[302]

More significantly, Muslims who want to change the narrative in the culture at large have concluded that the best way to do it is to produce their own material. Accordingly, there is a wellspring of pro-Islam and mockingly anti-Islam material being written and launched in the form of stand-up comedy, print comics and independent films.[303] Hollywood professionals who are anti-Jihad and oppose the Islamic supremacist movement might consider mimicking this technique in film, comedy, and the culture at large.

Hollywood Actors: Siding with the Enemy

In addition to the issue of Hollywood's Muslim and Arab actors protesting so-called "stereotypes," several non-Muslim celebrity actors are taking the issue a step further by publicly championing the cause of Islam.

Ben Affleck

For example, in October of 2014, on comedian Bill Maher's HBO show "Real Time," Ben Affleck lost his composure defending Islam and Muslims. Bill Maher correctly asserted, "Liberals need to stand up for liberal principles…. like freedom of speech, freedom to practice any religion you want without fear of violence, freedom to leave a religion, equality for women, equality for homosexuals. These are liberal values." But, he went on, "when you point out that these values are absent in the Muslim world, people get upset."[304]

Actor Sam Harris explained that people have bought into the idea that every criticism of Islamic doctrine (ideas) is "Islamophobic" and is incorrectly conflated with criticism of Muslims (people). Ben Affleck interjected, visibly agitated, asking, "Are you the one who understands the officially codified doctrine of Islam?" Harris argued, "We have to be able to criticize bad ideas. Islam is the motherload of bad ideas."

Barely able to contain himself, Affleck insisted that more than a billion Muslims don't want to [kill people or commit terrorism]; it's just "stereotyping." He characterized Harris' and Maher's comments as "gross" and "racist."[305] Though some of the confusion appeared to be due to a conflation of Islamic doctrine (ideas) with those who identify themselves as Muslim (people), Maher and Harris correctly pointed out that it is not just the doctrine that is problematic, but the people who believe in the doctrine.[306]

Ben Affleck, who won both Academy and Golden Globe Awards for producing and directing the film "Argo" about Iranian hostages (among other numerous awards and nominations over the years),[307] came from an ultra-liberal household. Born in Berkeley, California, he confesses that he was raised in a "union household" with parents who were "far left-wing Democrats."

Affleck admits that he has carried the values of his childhood into adulthood and into Hollywood. He has campaigned and supported numerous far-left politicians, has attended fundraisers[308] for Democrats and made numerous political donations.[309] Some of the politicians he has supported include but are not limited to the far left-wing politicians Maxine Waters, Barbara Boxer,[310] Elizabeth Warren and Richard Gephardt.[311]

Michael Moore

Shortly after the San Bernardino Islamic terrorist attack in December, 2015, producer and director Michael Moore was seen in front of Trump Towers holding a large sign which read, "We are all Muslim Now."[312] In response to then-Presidential candidate Donald Trump's call for a temporary travel ban on Muslims until the government can properly vet them, Michael Moore went into a rage. A far leftist for the entirety of his Hollywood career, Michael Moore's website tells the viewer much more about his politics than his movies.[313] Failing or refusing to understand that Islam is not like other religions, and that the problem is more than a few bad apples who happen to be Muslim, Michael Moore posted a letter to Donald Trump accusing him of being an "angry white guy" who is looking for Muslim "boogeymen" in corners where they do not exist.[314]

Stated Moore:

"We are all Muslim. Just as we are all Mexican, we are all Catholic and Jewish and white and black and every shade in between. We are all children of God (or nature or whatever you believe in), part of the human family, and nothing you say or do can change that fact one iota. If you don't like living by these American rules, then you need to go to the time-out room in any one of your Towers, sit there, and think about what you've said."[315]

Subsequently, Moore encouraged others to take photos of themselves holding signs saying "We are all Muslim" and post them on their Facebook and Twitter accounts.[316]

Yet, Michael Moore, like other leftists in Hollywood, turns a blind eye to the fact that Islam inherently contradicts all the values of equality and minority rights that he professes to embrace.[317] MPAC's Hollywood Bureau bestowed an award upon Michael Moore for showing Muslims in a positive light.[318] How apropos.

Richard Gere

In the wake of the terrorist attacks of September 11, 2001, actor Richard Gere, who is a practicing Buddhist,[319] spoke to a packed crowd at a benefit concert for 9/11 victims in New York City's Central Park. He told them that we must not take revenge, but show the terrorists love. [320] Even for the undoubtedly left-leaning audience, this over the top statement was met with loud shouts of "boo!"[321] "I guess that's not a popular idea right now," Gere replied.

In 2005, Gere appeared in a commercial encouraging Palestinians in Gaza to vote. "Hi, I'm Richard Gere and I'm speaking for the entire world. We're with you during this election time. It's really important: Get out and vote."[322] Yet, this act, which was intended to be supportive, drew the ire of many Palestinians who subsequently complained that they hated Richard Gere even more than they hated then-Israeli Prime Minister Ariel Sharon.[323]

In later years, Gere proclaimed that he wanted to do something to counter the "Innocence of Muslims" film[324] (which was falsely touted by then-Secretary of State Hillary Clinton, as the cause of a "spontaneous" uprising at Benghazi). [325] It's unclear whether or not Gere's unpopularity among Palestinian Muslims and the wrath they expressed toward him played a role in Gere's subsequent quest to find a role in a film which portrayed Islam in a positive light.

Additional "Progressive" Celebrities Who Apologize for Islam

In the meantime, other Hollywood celebrities, simply because of their far left bent or out of ignorance, seem to find common cause with Islam, consistently finding conservatives rather than Islamic terrorists, to be the ultimate enemy.

A case in point is Sean Penn, who jokingly accused former President George Bush and Vice President Dick Cheney of "inventing" ISIS.[326]

Rosie O'Donnell, famous comedienne and 9/11 Truther, believes that the cause of Islamic jihad is not Islamic religious doctrine, but anti-Muslim bias. To support her claim, she cited the fact that the NFL penalized a player for Islamic prayers made during a football game. This "propels us to war," she proclaimed.[327]

Yusuf Islam, the musician formerly known as Cat Stevens, while not a Hollywood actor himself, is certainly a big draw amongst the Hollywood crowd. When the British pop-singer converted to Islam in 1977 at the height of his career, he initially gave up music entirely, believing it to be un-Islamic.[328] He also turned down a recording contract and gave away all his guitars.[329] He used the wealth he acquired in the music industry to found the first full-time Islamic primary school in Britain,[330] and then later established some Islamic secondary schools as well.[331]

Yusuf Islam was placed on the U.S. terror no-fly list after being deported from Israel for donating money to Hamas.[332] He also supported the notion that author Salman Rushdie deserved to die for violating Islamic blasphemy rules.[333] Yet, Yusuf Islam was perplexed as to why people blamed him for his views. After all, he noted, that's what Islam calls for and he was merely explaining it.[334] Asked if he would participate in burning an effigy of Salman Rushdie, he replied, "I would have hoped that it'd be the real thing."[335]

In 2006, Yusuf Islam's ban from entry into the U.S was lifted.[336] In the 1990's, Yusuf Islam gradually started playing music again, at first restricting himself to Islamic music, [337] but later expanding outwards. In 2014, he was inducted into the Hall of Fame. In October, 2016, Yusuf Islam performed a concert in Hollywood, Los Angeles at the Pentages Theatre[338] as part of his first North American tour in years.[339] A percentage of the ticket profits went to Muslim refugees through Yusuf Islam's "charity" called "Small Kindness."[340] It should be noted that it was Yusuf Islam's prior "charitable donations" that got him in trouble in the first place, because his prior donations supported Hamas terrorism.

The Oscar Award Ceremony and the Red-Green Axis

Islamists and the far Left have increasingly joined forces to undermine the Judeo-Christian values that serve as the underpinning of American freedom. Presumably, under the theory that the enemy of my enemy is my friend, groups emanating from Marxist-communist or socialist foundations (the Red Axis) and groups which have ties to the Muslim Brotherhood and/or Islamic terrorist groups (the Green Axis), align to destroy their common Enemies, namely America and Israel.[341] The Red-Green Axis manifests itself perfectly in Hollywood, as was evidenced during the 2017 Oscar Award Ceremony.

The Oscar Award Ceremony is ostensibly about recognizing artistic and technical excellence in the film industry, is hosted by the Academy of Motion Picture Arts and Science, and is televised annually.[342] Yet, during the 89th Oscar Ceremony in February of 2017, the entire show was replete with political jabs against the newly elected President Trump. The digs were aimed largely at the President's positions regarding immigration and refugees, including his Executive Order, which was mischaracterized as a "Muslim Ban."[343]

In point of fact, the Executive Order wasn't religiously based, nor was it a permanent ban.[344] Rather, it was a temporary pause of the influx of refugees from all religious backgrounds if they came from one of seven countries that are either failed states, demonstrate inability to secure management of key documents like passports, and/or had a high risk of terrorism. These countries had previously been identified by President Obama as countries of concern.[345] All of this was blatantly disregarded at the Oscars.

To kick off the event, in his opening statement, TV talk show host Jimmy Kimmel made numerous statements intimating that Trump's policies were "racist and discriminatory," laughing that at least in Hollywood they don't discriminate based on race, just weight and age. [346]

The elites at the Oscars turned the awards show into a platform for leftist political commentary to such an extent that some weren't adequately focused on properly delivering the awards. As a result, Warren Beatty and Faye Dunaway were handed the wrong envelope and wound up incorrectly announcing that "Lala Land" won the "Best Picture" Award, when the rightful winner of the award was "Moonlight."[347]

The winner of the Best Documentary Short was "White Helmets," about saving victims of the Syrian war. The producer read a statement from one of the Muslim rescue workers in Syria, which misquoted the Qur'an, saying "to save one life is the save all humanity."[348] Never mind that the accurate quote is "[I]f you save one life, you save the whole world" and that though it was cited in the Qur'an centuries later, its origin is the Jewish Talmud.[349]

Moreover, recently, five film directors had signed a declaration purportedly on behalf of all nominees expressing "unanimous and emphatic disapproval of the climate of nationalism and fanaticism." They lauded "diversity of cultures" and criticized those who advocate for "divisive walls" that categorize based on "genders, colors, religions and sexualities."[350]

Of course, these statements were based on the false equation of prioritizing "America First" (which is part of American exceptionalism), with the abhorrent and discriminatory concepts of racism and bigotry. The statements also emanate from the concept of "intersectionality,"[351] a leftist social theory which erroneously asserts that to be bigoted toward one group, once must necessarily be "bigoted" toward other minority groups as well. Intersectionality leaves no room for legitimate concerns stemming from hostile ideologies. Instead, it assumes that all values are equal and therefore antipathy toward those with hostile intent counts as "bigotry."[352]

Without question though, the center of attention during the Oscar Awards Ceremony was an Iranian Film Director named Asghar Farhadi, who won an award for the Best Foreign Language Film, "The Salesman."[353]

Back in January, Farhadi had announced that he would boycott the awards ceremony in protest of Trump's travel ban, despite the fact that the Trump Administration gave Farhadi clearance to come directly to America in order to attend the Awards show.[354] Farhadi's statement drew a lot of press attention and perhaps even tipped the scales in favor of him winning the often politically motivated awards.[355] Purportedly in support of Farhadi, the Academy of Motion Picture Arts and Sciences, which hosts the annual Oscar Ceremony, came out with an official statement condemning Trump's Executive Order.[356]

In his absence, Farhadi had Anousheh Ansari, the first Muslim woman to travel in space, read his acceptance speech at the Oscars. In it, Farhadi claimed that the reason he refused to attend the Oscars was out of respect for those from his country and the other six countries listed in Trump's Executive Order who were "disrespected in the inhumane law that bans entry of immigrants to the U.S." Farhadi went on to say that "dividing the world into the 'U.S. and our enemies' categories creates fear, a deceitful justification of aggression and war... These wars in turn prevent democracy and human rights in countries which have themselves been the victims of aggression." He then called for filmmakers to write and produce films that elicit "empathy between cultures" and make films that "break religious stereotypes."[357]

Clearly, Farhadi is confusing cause with effect. According to him, it is America's labeling of terror-prone countries as the enemy which causes them to become our enemies, rather than terrorism that causes America to label these countries as enemies. Farhadi's argument implies that somehow it is America's fault that Islamic countries don't have human rights, ignoring the fact that America has done nothing to prevent human rights from being implemented, and more importantly, the countries in question have taken no action demonstrating an interest in human rights. Yet, the Islamic world is ever the victim.

Farhadi's plea was for film-makers to change their narratives rather than to explore the facts or express a range of views. He clearly has a pre-determined outcome in mind. It's hard to know whether or not his statements were consciously intended as da'wa, but there is no doubt that if Farhadi gets his way, the result will be the same: to alter cultural and political belief systems through the use of film.

The United Voices Rally

Farhadi is a client of United Talent Agency or UTA, one of the most powerful talent agencies in the country. It usually holds an Oscar Awards celebration after the ceremony, but in 2017, UTA decided to cancel the party and hold a pro-immigration rally instead, claiming its support for Farhadi.[358]

The rally was dubbed "United Voices" and was held in Beverly Hills. Farhadi spoke at the rally via video, having refused to come to America subsequent to Trump's Travel Executive Order, despite White House permission to do so.[359]

UTA issued a press release asserting that the Executive Order has a "chilling effect on the global exchange of ideas, not to mention freedom of expression."[360]

Other liberal notables who spoke at the rally included: California Lieutenant Governor Gavin Newson, former UK Foreign Secretary David Miliband (who now heads the International Refugee Committee), and ACLU

Executive Director Hector Villagra, who encouraged everyone to "fight the Muslim Ban."[361]

Michael J. Fox[362] and Jodie Foster took the stage using nonsensical rhetoric that sounded nice but had no discernable meaning.[363] CNN's Reza Aslan (an Iranian-American Muslim and UTA client)[364] spoke, and Jeremy Zimmer, UTA's CEO, announced that he donated a quarter of a million dollars to the ACLU and the International Refugee Committee. He also started a CrowdRise fundraising site which raised 70,000 dollars to help refugees.[365]

The overriding message of the rally was "unity and resistance,"[366] bringing up images of the Nazi resistance in a brazen display of the Left's total inability to accept the presidential election results.

The London Screening

In London, the first Muslim Mayor of a Western Capitol city, Mayor Sadiq Khan, organized a free screening of Asghar Farhadi's film, demonstrating support for anti-Trump protests and proclaiming, "Trump can't silence me!"[367]

Thousands of people attended the screening. Farhadi, who accused Trump of building "divisive walls," spoke to the crowd via video, as did other Hollywood celebrities including Kiera Knightly, who likewise insisted that "racist and nationalist rhetoric is becoming political policy."[368]

The Mayor encouraged solidarity with Farhadi and "citizens around the world affected by discrimination based solely on their religion, country of origin or their birthplace." [369] Presumably, his statement was not referring to the legally mandated discrimination against Jews and Christians in Muslim majority countries governed by shariah.

Additional Subsequent Hollywood Events

There are numerous additional examples where Hollywood stars express unfettered sympathy for Muslims of all stripes and detestation for national security policies that would keep America safe from jihadists. It cannot be a coincidence that Hollywood celebrities voicing this sentiment also often demonstrate allegiance to partisan leftist politics.

For instance, in January 2017, at the Golden Globe Awards, Meryl Streep and other Hollywood actors lambasted President Trump's immigration and refugee policies.[370]

Another example was when actress Ashley Judd, star celeb at the Women's March against Trump on Capitol Hill, read in dramatic fashion, a poem written by a 19 year-old that reframed Trump's prior use of the term "nasty woman."[371]

While Hollywood has always leaned politically to the left, it is nevertheless evincing an unusually high level of Trump bashing. The Left, including Hollywood elites, seems obsessed with Trump's immigration, refugee, and America First policies,[372] which they purposely mischaracterize as having racist, Islamophobic,[373] or xenophobic intent.

Needless to say that the same Leftists who insist America should take in more refugees, often want nothing to do with them once they are here. They don't want to take refugees into their homes or have them settled in their own neighborhoods. Their unstated motto is "not in my backyard" (NIMBY).[374] But, they are perfectly happy to have refugees come to America into YOUR back yard.

The First Hollywood Iftar Dinner

MOST Arranges an Iftar Dinner for Hollywood

Hosted by MOST [375] and the Writers Guild Foundation, Hollywood experienced its first Iftar dinner on June 14, 2017. [376] Approximately 50 people attended.[377] The organizations invited a select group of writers and producers to attend, including high profile Hollywood elites from TV shows including "The Office," "Parks and Recreation," "Smallville," and "The Italian Job."[378]

ArabAmerica.com claimed that this "authentic Iftar" dinner would provide a "special opportunity" to express a "commitment" to "open public expression, freedom of travel, and free speech."[379] It appears that this phrase was written from the viewpoint of the Islamic ummah. Therefore, in context, "freedom to travel" arguably refers to the "freedom" to immigrate demanded by Muslim "refugees" and migrants.[380] Presumably, it's not a call for women in restrictive Islamic countries such as Saudi Arabia to be unshackled from the prohibitions to leave their country without their husbands' permission or to leave their homes without a male escort. [381] Similarly, "freedom of speech" from an Islamic point of view excludes blasphemy and so-called "religious insult." This stands in direct contrast to the First Amendment's concept of free speech in which political and religious ideas properly remain open to scrutiny and criticism, as part of protected speech.[382]

The Two Faces of Ramadan

The Eid al-Fitr holiday marks the end of the Islamic holy month of Ramadan, during which Muslims fast during the day, but are permitted to eat after sundown. The holiday is presented as commemorating the Muslims' commitment to the Qur'an, [383] the teachings of the Muslim Prophet Muhammad, gratitude to Allah, and empathy with the poor. [384] In fact, of course, the Eid al-Fitr marks the Battle of Badr fought in 624 CE, which was the first time that Muslim forces defeated non-Muslims on the field of battle. In keeping with that historical event, and because Islam is a supremacist political religion, the month of Ramadan routinely also bears witness to an increase in violent jihad across the globe.[385] Despite Islam's distinction from non-political religions, UPF and MOST overtly tried to conflate the teachings of Judaism and Christianity with those of Islam, in using this holiday as a solicitation to fundraise. [386]

An Opportunity For Influence

The event stressed the importance of "sharing Muslim stories" and lumped all religions together, on the false assumption that they have shared values. Ignoring the fact that those born into Islam risk the death penalty mandated under shariah if they decide to leave,[387] UPF's introductory remarks asserted that "[R]eligion can be meaningful when it's a personal choice."[388]

Jawaad Abdul Rahman (UPF Producer and Development Director), asserted that the United States as a society needs to better understand Ramadan and the Muslim holiday of Eid al-Fitr. He applauded the "fastathons" which are beginning to take place in North America in celebration of Ramadan, engaged in by both Muslims and non-Muslims alike.[389]

Additionally, the UPF introductory remarks asserted that the muezzin or prayer caller clasps his hands in prayer and says "Allahu Akbar," which was translated as "God is greater." [390] But, if "God is greater," then whom is he greater than? The answer, conveniently omitted in the UPF remarks, is that that Allah, (the Muslim's God) is greater than the God of Judaism, Christianity or other religions. Remember: warriors and soldiers of Allah shout this out prior to every murder, terrorist attack and beheading they commit.[391]

Conflating the Abrahamic Faiths

In a classic act of Da'wa, speakers from UPF's team likened the Ramadan fast to the fasts of Yom Kippur and Lent. They discussed the connection of Islam's prayers to Moses, Jesus and Muhammad, claiming they all came with the same message as part of the Abrahamic faith.[392] This is often a ploy to appeal to non-Muslims and convince them that their belief systems share much more in common with Islam than they really do. The speakers conveniently omitted, (as those who engage in Da'wa propaganda always do,) that Islam claims all the Prophets prior to the birth of Muhammad were also Muslim – including Moses and Jesus,[393] whose Divinity Islam denies.[394]

A Plea for Hollywood's Capitulation

MOST boasted of acting as a consultant for famed Hollywood TV shows including "Grey's Anatomy," "The Good Wife," "Army Wives," and "Bones." Michael Wolfe (MOST Co-Director and UPF Executive Director) made an appeal to the audience members' egos, inviting them to have "courage." In essence, he asked them to work to effectuate social change on behalf of Muslims, despite his quasi-acknowledgement that it's not their job. He stated, "I know you are not in the social change business, *but* [emphasis added] ... you can and do make an enormous difference."[395]

The UPF introductory remarks called on the audience to "humanize" Muslims, to "break stereotypes" and close the gap between "us and them."[396] Muslims were also painted as victims to both American culture and "extremist groups" abroad[397] (referring to Islamic terrorist groups).

Analysis of the Hollywood-Islamist Alliance: The Trump Effect

Until Trump appeared on the scene, Hollywood's support of the Muslim community and its causes were initiated in large part, by Muslim groups. There was less of a push emanating from Hollywood professionals to join forces with Islamists than one would expect. Actors, directors and producers, for the most part, though, still seemed happy to make common cause with Islam when the impetus originated from Muslim organizations. Now, with a Trump presidency, much of the Left, including elements of Hollywood, has become unhinged, especially with regard to the Administration's stance on Islamic terrorism, its underlying ideology, and Trump's determination to keep jihadists out of the country.

Hollywood's motives for complicity in supporting Islamists can be partly attributed to appeasement and naïveté, but mostly it's part and parcel of the broader unholy alliance between Islamic supremacists and far-leftists. This alliance constitutes a movement to criticize, condemn, and undermine the traditional Judeo-Christian values upon which America was built, but to keep shariah criticism-free. The alliance is comprised of Muslim Brotherhood front-groups such as CAIR, like-minded Islamic supremacist groups such UPF's MOST, as well as the Black Lives Matter movement and the interfaith dialogue movement.

Disguised in the language of "minority rights," "civil rights," "multiculturalism" and "inclusiveness," these unlikely bed-fellows join forces to alter the narrative in the West and change America's cultural climate through use of the media and other societal institutions. Under the theory that "the enemy of my enemy is my friend," Islamic supremacists and far-left "progressives" work together to subvert America as we know it and make room for the creation of a Utopia that will never be.[398]

CHAPTER 9

INROADS AT INDEPENDENT FILM FESTIVALS

Propagating Anti-Israel Films

More and more often, Muslims and far-leftists are aligning for the purpose of demonizing Israel and delegitimizing her right to exist as a Jewish state. Anti-Israel "documentaries" help fuel hatred against Israel and give rise to antisemitic sentiment.

Indeed, many Muslims consider America "The Great Satan" and consider Israel "The Little Satan."[399] And though in the past, Israel garnered bi-partisan support, in recent years, the Democrat party has pulled away from several of its pro-Israel positions.[400] In the "social justice" movement and "progressive" circles, anti-Israel sentiment has become commonplace, even fashionable, especially on college campuses, which have become centers for liberal indoctrination.[401]

During the annual "Apartheid Week," universities around the country provide a venue for anti-Israel views,[402] bashing Israel, despite the fact that it is the only free country in the Middle East. Apartheid week activities include one-sided "documentaries" that portray Israel as evil. Additionally, universities are used as venues in which to hold panels, events, and disseminate of literature containing an anti-Israel bent. Generally, the claim emanating from the films and lectures is that Israel is committing "ethnic genocide," "war crimes" or "human rights violations."[403] Efforts to express countering views are silenced, intimidated or otherwise discouraged.

Sometimes, the anti-Israel position expressed during Apartheid Week is really a mask for antisemitism.[404] It is not yet socially acceptable to openly express hatred of Jews on college campuses. Therefore, antisemitic hatred is couched in terms of delegitimizing Israel, the only Jewish State on earth, representing the "collective Jew." [405] Increasingly, however, the antisemitism is becoming unmasked, outwardly demonstrated in screaming matches and physical harassment of Jews on college campuses. [406]

There are also film festivals and other arenas where anti-Israel films are shown, usually in the form of independent "documentaries." For example, the DC Palestinian Film and Arts Festival in 2015 featured a film given the "Best Documentary Film Award" at Michael Moore's Traverse City Film Festival.[407] The San Francisco University also held a film festival on the so-called "Israel-Palestine conflict," displaying anti-Israel hatred and bias.[408]

Muslim Film Festivals

A Da'wa Mission

Increasingly, Muslim film festivals are being launched into the mainstream public sphere featuring films that are characterized as "anti-war," "pro-Islam," or "pro-Palestinian." Alternatively, the films will reflect a Muslim-African-American alliance. These festivals are popping up all over the country including cities such as Philadelphia, Boston, and Milwaukee. They are also being held on college campuses.[409] In addition to Muslim film festivals, pro-Islam films are finding their way into foreign film festivals, Arab film festivals and other independent film festivals.[410]

Muslim film festivals are undoubtedly part of a larger Da'wa mission to address issues of concern to Muslims, primarily within the realm of politics.[411] The movies shown target a Muslim audience, and garner support from myriad Muslim organizations, many of which are Muslim Brotherhood front-groups. The festivals encourage film submissions from Muslim filmmakers and would-be filmmakers.[412] The films are often accompanied by panel discussions or other activities, sometimes even featuring "red carpet" events.[413] The purpose of the films is to indoctrinate Muslim audiences in an effort to unify the Islamic ummah[414] on relevant political issues. Films range from "underground films" produced by emerging Muslim filmmakers to Oscar-nominated movies.[415]

An Al-Qaeda "Child"

For example, the Milwaukee Film Festival 2016 featured the films "Journey into Europe," "Guantanamo's Child: Omar Khadr" and "Prison Blues." Guantanamo's Child portrays the journey of Al-Qaeda terrorist during his stay at Guantanamo prison. Despite Khadr's terrorist ties and conviction for killing an American, this film is sympathetic to Khadr. Though the film does not dispute Khadr's actions, it argues that he was wrongfully jailed simply because at age 15, he was merely "a child soldier" when captured in

Afghanistan by the U.S. military.[416] Here, as in many of the other films shown during these festivals, terrorists and common criminals including murderers, are portrayed as victims.

It is interesting to note that subsequently, the Canadian government awarded Khadr a 10.5 million dollar settlement in a lawsuit he filed for the time he spent in Guantanamo and his treatment while there. The settlement appears to have been agreed to by the Canadian government, at least in part, to evade the higher costs of litigation and does not deny the criminal acts for which he was charged. [417]

Jailing "Victims"

A similar victimhood mentality weaves throughout the film "Prison Blues." This film starts by citing misleading statistics, which are often mirror comments by leftist politicians. Falsely implying that those of all races commit crimes in the same percentages, the film cites that blacks constitute only 12 percent of the population, yet constitute 40 percent of the prison population. [418] The implied conclusion is that the prison population should reflect race percentages within the general population rather than the race percentages of the criminal population.

Showing what appears to be a staged arrest of a very young black boy, in addition to obviously dated black and white footage of arrests made presumably before the Civil Rights Act, this "documentary" treats the 1950's as though it were 2016 in a transparent attempt to rile people up. The movie films felons with sentences ranging from 14 to 20 years for unnamed crimes, portraying them as victims who have found solace in Islam.[419]

"Prison Blues" encourages Muslims to accept blacks into their communities. It demonstrates the brotherhood of Islam that exists behind prison bars. Telling stories that could only be moving to naïve bleeding hearts, this film boasts that Islam can take a hardened murderer and turn him into a chivalrous gentleman.

Such was the path of one felon, who, according to the film, became so warm-hearted that he actually gave someone who was crying a tissue without wanting credit for it.[420] Apparently, the film-maker thought this was a praise-worthy achievement, despite the fact that to most people, this unheroic act would be considered unworthy of mention.

In the end, the film makes a plea for the call to Da'wa, to assist in the growth of the Islamic movement. The film correctly points out that the movement has grown in prisons nationwide, where 80 percent of inmates who "come to faith" are converts to Islam.[421] It is no coincidence that the

Milwaukee film Festival is sponsored in part by the Muslim Student Association and the Islamic Society of Milwaukee, [422] both of which are Muslim Brotherhood affiliates.

Spreading Propaganda

Additional Islamic propaganda films fill the theaters at the annual Milwaukee Muslim Film Festival and other Muslim film festivals around the country. One example can be found at ISNA's annual convention, where it hosts a film festival, among other activities. [423] Films shown here include "documentaries," "historical films" "educational films" and "religious or inspirational films," as well as comedies and dramas.[424]

Islamic Blasphemy: "Dangerous" Speech

Years ago, ISNA showed a film titled "Blastphemy," accompanied by a presentation by Dalia Mogahed,[425] a well-known Islamic apologist. Shown after the publishing of the infamous Danish cartoons of the Muslim Prophet Muhammad which sparked riots throughout the Middle East and Denmark, this "documentary" intended to demonstrate the dangers of publishing drawings deemed offensive in Islam. With interviews of Dalia Mogahed, Imam Siraj Wahhaj (a named unindicted co-conspirator in the 1993 World Trade Center bombing)[426] and others, the interviewees, in effect, argued for censorship of speech or cartoons that violate Islamic blasphemy laws.

Repeatedly, interviewees insisted that such offense does not constitute free speech but "hate mongering" that "endangers the lives" of Muslims in the West,[427] despite the fact that there is no evidence to support this contention. [428]

Moreover, under America's First Amendment, there is no right to be free from insult, religious or otherwise. The Judeo-Christian values upon which this country was founded, as well as U.S. laws, mandate that those who are violent take personal responsibility and are held accountable for their behavior. This film attempted to shift responsibility from those who are violent to those who made "offensive" comments. Since the interviewees did not recommend equal censorship for insults against other religions such as Judaism or Christianity, this film effectively advocated a position of preferential treatment of Islam.

The Proliferation of Muslim Film Festivals

Additional Muslim Film Festivals in the U.S. include the Boston Film Festival, the Muslim Youth Voices Project which creates films for a film festival in Philadelphia,[429] and the Muslim Film Festival (MFF) which took place at University of California, at the Berkeley and Santa Clara campuses.[430]

Similar film festivals can be found in Europe and Canada, such as "The Mosquers," held in Edmonton, Canada, where the festival's sponsors were fairly candid about their goal to "transform the way people see Muslims."[431]

Analysis: Why Indie Films?

Producing films by Muslims for Muslims is the first step within the movie-making industry to unify the voice of the Islamic Ummah. In an attempt to create the feeling of "brotherhood" and "community," these independent films provide an opportunity for Muslims who have anti-American, anti-Israel, and anti-national security sentiments to express themselves in a creative outlet with sympathetic audiences.

Muslims are always the first target for the Muslim Brotherhood organizations that seek to galvanize the masses and unite them for the cause of Islamic supremacy. [432]

Ironically, this is achieved in part by creating an "us versus them" mentality, a tactic that the Islamist-leftist alliance often accuses the right of engaging in. Islamic groups consistently portray Muslims as victims, often claiming that when Islamic terrorists are imprisoned, it is due to "stereotyping," "discrimination" or simply "because of their religion."[433]

Once Muslims are on board with this narrative in mass numbers, they can participate in the implementation of additional next steps. These include disarming the public through interfaith programs, disinformation-based "education" campaigns, and insisting that Islamic terrorism has nothing to do with the "true" Islam, which Muslim Brotherhood groups claim is a religion of "peace" despite all the evidence to the contrary.

CHAPTER 10

PROTESTING PRO-AMERICAN FILMS

Background: America is the Enemy

In addition to persuading audiences to believe in the harmlessness of Islam, several Muslim groups appear to be intent on bashing any film that portrays America as strong in her fight against Islamic terrorism. Denouncing American heroes such as Navy Seal Chris Kyle as cold-blooded anti-Muslim murderers, groups like CAIR, the Muslim Students Association (another Muslim Brotherhood affiliate), and the American-Arab Anti-Discrimination Committee (ADC) lead the charge to cancel screenings of patriotic films that take place within a war context.

Example: *American Sniper*

The film *American Sniper*, directed by Clint Eastwood and starring Bradley Cooper, is based on a true story about U.S. Navy SEAL Chris Kyle. This sniper was an American hero who saved countless American lives on the battlefield during the Iraq war. His incredible aim and shooting skills earned him the nickname "Legend." When not fighting in war, he did all he could to try to help those who needed him. But in the end, he was killed off the battlefield by someone who betrayed him, leaving his wife without a husband and his children without a father.[434]

The film documents armed U.S. forces fighting Iraqi terrorists led by Abu Musab al Zarqawi. It in no way generalizes the negative portrayals of Islamic terrorists to all Muslims. [435] Still, Muslim Brotherhood affiliates persisted in false accusations of stereotyping Muslims.

American Sniper was one of the most successful box office hits in America and the number one wartime film in history. It shattered box office records in its opening weekend,[436] and grossed over 337 million dollars in 2014, making it the highest grossing film in America that year.[437] Within a year and a half, it grossed 547 million dollars internationally.[438] The film appealed to a wide range of audiences,[439] was nominated for six Academy Award nominations,[440] won an Oscar for its sound editing.[441] Yet, groups like the Muslim Student Association (MSA), CAIR, and the American-Arab Anti-Discrimination Committee (ADC) didn't want the public to see it.

At the University of Maryland, the MSA started a petition to cancel a scheduled screening of *American Sniper.* The petition claimed that the film was "Islamophobic," "racist," "offensive to many Muslims," "dehumanizes Muslim individuals, promotes the idea of senseless murder, and portrays negative and inaccurate stereotypes."[442] In an Orwellian reversal of language definitions, the petition requested Student Entertainment Events (SEE) to: "exercise your freedom of speech to help us create a safer campus environment" by censoring the film to "create a more inclusive and diverse community atmosphere."[443]

SEE capitulated to MSA's demands while still pretending to support freedom of speech. Fortunately, in response, the College Democrats and College Republicans agreed to jointly sponsor a screening on campus.[444]

East Michigan University planned to show two screenings of *American Sniper* on a Friday night. During the first viewing, thirty-five protestors marched on stage to disrupt the evening. The protest leaders, Ahmed Abbas, Layali Alsadah, Jenna Hamed, and Sabreen Dari were arrested. Subsequently, the movie resumed. The second viewing was cancelled however, but promised to be shown at a later date.[445]

One of the protest leaders, Ahmad Abbas, somehow believes that he has the right to interrupt a film viewing and protest a screening without his protest being criticized. Regarding criticism launched against him, he asserted, "This is not about freedom of speech, this is not about freedom of expression, this is about public safety and people being respected with dignity ... that's why we're here. If you want to voice yourself, students shouldn't be protesting" (meaning that the protestors shouldn't be protested). And yet, it was Abbas' protestors who potentially put the safety of the movie watchers at risk.[446]

Ironically, one of Abbas' protestors held up a sign which read, "is this your idea of dialogue?"[447] Apparently, that protestor's idea of "dialogue" was shutting down a popular movie to prevent viewers from receiving the film's information.

Fortunately, not everyone has caved in to Islamist demands to censor *American Sniper.* Clint Eastwood and Bradley Cooper became targets of the American Anti-Discrimination Committee (AAD), which claimed that the film villainizes Muslims and puts their lives at risk. They argued that the movie endangers Muslims, and they pled with the producer and actor to help alleviate the "danger" by denouncing "hateful rhetoric" against Muslims. To their credit, neither Eastwood nor Cooper capitulated.[448]

Similarly, the University of Missouri made a decision to ignore the cries of Muslim activist and psychology/gender studies major, Farah El-Jayyous. EL-Jayyous whined that showing the film on campus would make her feel "unsafe" and would "create an even more hostile environment for me and other Arab, Muslim, South Asian and people of color. ..." Labeling the film "racist," El-Jayyous claimed that her letter was "not an attempt at censorship, but an affirmation of my right to feel safe ... freedom of speech should not come at the expense of anyone's humanity and right to be viewed, talked about and treated with basic respect and dignity." In other words, she wants censorship.

Many other college campuses struggled with whether or not to show the film over the objections of Muslim Brotherhood front-groups. Some caved in while others stood stalwart.[449]

Example: *Dark Zero Thirty*

Dark Zero Thirty was a dramatization of the decade-long manhunt for Al-Qaeda's leader, Osama Bin Laden, after the 9/11 attacks. It was billed as "the story of history's greatest manhunt for the world's most dangerous man."[450] It starred Jessica Chastain in the underrepresented role of female CIA operative, and was released worldwide in January 2013.[451]

Though it won several awards and was nominated for even more,[452] it drew the ire of many left-wing groups that couched the film as a "pro-torture" movie. Disregarding the fact that many of the controversial techniques such as water-boarding are conducted on Navy SEALs as part of their training,[453] and sticking their heads in the sand to the greater evil that would ensue if Al-Qaeda's top leaders were permitted to live and carry out additional plans to murder infidel Westerners, groups like the "National Religious Campaign Against Torture" and "Interfaith Communities United for Justice and Peace" organized in Hollywood to protest the film.[454]

Ironically, the film makers, Kathryn Bowman and Mark Boal, who won an Oscar Award for *Hurt Locker* the previous year, went out of their way to ensure that *Dark Zero Thirty* was not released before President Obama had the chance to be re-elected.[455] The movie received accolades by those on the right, but left wing and "progressive" film reviewers were "falling all over themselves" to denounce the film in numerous different ways.[456]

While the Award givers are to be commended for giving *Zero Dark Thirty* credit where it was due, film critics and their elitist friends in Hollywood still lambasted the film.[457]

CHAPTER 11

RECOMMENDATIONS

I n order to inoculate ourselves against the dangerous influence of Islamic supremacists, the U.S. government, interfaith groups, and the public must join forces, mobilize and become active. People across the political spectrum must recognize the dangers of Islamic supremacism and unite to fight against its subversion of American freedom and security before it's too late.

What Individuals Can Do:

1) "An informed citizenry is the best defense to freedom." Every day citizens should start by educating themselves, their families, their friends and neighbors. Bring a friend to a speaker event, pass along an article, or discuss current events at the dinner table. If everyone does just one thing a week, it will have a ripple effect.

2) Church congregations should try to persuade their pastors to refrain from participating in interfaith programs. At a minimum, all program participants should be thoroughly vetted to ensure that they don't have any affiliations with terrorist groups or Muslim Brotherhood front-groups, and that they do not share shariah's inegalitarian, anti-freedom ideology or aspirations.

3) Parents should monitor their children's school text books for falsehoods on Islamic theology and history, and pay attention to school events indoctrinating students or giving preference to Islam, such as "wear a hijab day" or field trips to mosques.

4) Most of all, instill in your children the ability to think critically and question what they are taught, whether it's in school, in a "documentary" or elsewhere. Students should also be introduced to alternative sources of information, and taught to conduct research on their own, rather than accepting one-sided positions at face value.

As a Society:

1) It is incumbent upon all of us to understand the Enemy Threat Doctrine asserted by the famous Chinese Military General, Sun Tzu, which requires that we know ourselves and know our Enemy. [458] Society must relinquish political correctness in favor of unpleasant truths.

2) We must acknowledge that political correctness is aiding and abetting our enemies. We must realize that academia, religious institutions, books, social media and Hollywood influences younger generations. We must act accordingly if we want a strong and free America.

3) It is imperative that we reconnect with the history of this great country and the Founding Principles on which it was founded, that allowed us to flourish in freedom and prosperity, rather than indoctrinate our youth with anti-American sentiment, which Islamic supremacists are taking full advantage of.

4) We must be clear on the facts. We cannot allow the leftist-Islamist alliance to fog the war by redefining words, using vague language or propagating false narratives. We must not cede control over our lexicon or reported facts.

5) We must value moral clarity. We must relinquish the fantasy that multiculturalism works and that all values are equal. We must not be afraid to assert that the Judeo-Christian values of freedom, equality and human rights are superior to Islamist values of institutionalized discrimination, tyranny and human rights abuses.

6) We must stop extending "tolerance" to those who don't have tolerance as a foundation for their own belief system. We should stop pretending that we can co-exist with an Enemy that has supremacist and inegalitarian ideals.

To Hollywood and Those in the Arts:

1) Those with the means and capability should produce their own films exposing Muslim Brotherhood front-groups and their political aspirations in the form of independent films and documentaries.

2) Producers should mimic the tactics of the Muslim Brotherhood and produce comic films to mock those who have fabricated the "Islamophobia" industry in an effort to delegitimize those who are concerned with Islamic terrorism, Islamic persecution of religious minorities and human rights violations committed in the name of Islam.

3) Artists, producers and script writers should learn to think critically and educate themselves before jumping on the bandwagon of political correctness when producing films.

4) Where possible, individuals and organizations who work on anti-shariah and national security-related issues should act in a consulting capacity to those in Hollywood and the film-making industry, especially to counteract the damage being caused by propaganda and disinformation campaigns waged by Islamic supremacist organizations.

5) Artists and film makers who care about national security should make a point to attend movie premiers and discussion groups that exhibit a pro-Islam tilt to raise appropriate questions and issues during question and answer periods. Better yet, try to book a representative on the discussion panels who will bring a different viewpoint.

What the U.S. Government Should Do:

1) The U.S. government, law enforcement, and national security apparatus should cut all ties with Muslim Brotherhood front-groups and those who are like-minded to stop giving them legitimacy. Agencies should stop collaborating with these groups and cease taking their advice. Government officials should refrain from delivering speeches at events hosted by Muslim Brotherhood affiliates. Government agencies should stop participating in their conferences in all capacities including setting up information and recruitment booths.

2) All government agencies and law enforcement must stop receiving "sensitivity training" and "cross-cultural training" from Muslim Brotherhood front groups and other Islamic supremacist organizations. Organizations that deliver these "training" programs should not receive the benefit of the GAO's seal of approval for government contracts. It is outrageous that we have all allowed Islamic supremacist groups to dictate how America handles national security and law enforcement. It is even worse that several agencies are getting "training" from groups that often oppose anti-terrorism efforts.

3) Our law enforcement agencies should persist in using training films on jihad that they deem educational, regardless of CAIR's protests. Under no circumstances should these films be replaced with "multi-cultural sensitivity" or "cross-cultural sensitivity" indoctrination that will inevitably lead to weakened protections of U.S. citizens.

4) Government agencies should not be taking national security advice from those who have ties to Islamic supremacist groups or share their ideology or aspirations. Government officials must learn not to take so-called "moderate" Muslim groups at face value. Instead, officials must become educated on the Muslim Brotherhood's strategies for civilization jihad as outlined in its 1991 Explanatory Memorandum and act accordingly.

5) There remains some measure of support for Congress to pass a bill to encourage the State Department to designate the Muslim Brotherhood as a foreign terrorist organization. An example of such a bill has been proposed by Senator Ted Cruz of Texas (S. 2230, Muslim Brotherhood Terrorist Designation Act of 2015). [459] If passed, it would rest with the President whether or not to direct the State Department to make the designation to the FTO list.

6) It is imperative that all branches of government start taking the War of Ideas seriously. The ideological battle must be made a priority and our government must approach it from the standpoint of America's best interests, rather than continually appeasing our enemies.

7) America needs a complete overhaul in the way we conceptualize and approach the war, our ideological enemies, and our interactions both militarily and diplomatically. We must properly distinguish our

friends from our enemies, rewarding allies and punishing foes, rather than do the opposite. America has the right and the obligation to protect the security, safety and freedom of our citizens. Our elected and appointed officials must prioritize U.S. interests, placing long term freedom above short term political expediency.

As President Reagan said, "[F]reedom is never more than one generation away from extinction."[460] America must muster up the willingness and the fortitude to place national security above political correctness. We must stand up for the Judeo-Christian principles of freedom and equality and put a stop to preferential treatment to those who would do us harm. We must be vigilant if we want to pass the torch of freedom to future generations.

CHAPTER 12

CONCLUSION

At a rally in front of the White House one year prior to 9/11, CAIR Executive Director Nihad Awad said, "Hollywood has not been our ally. ... Hollywood has shown freedom fighters as terrorists [referring to Hamas]. Hollywood has done the work that Zionists could not [have] done."[461]

But since 9/11, Hollywood has drastically changed.[462] The pattern in Hollywood films today denigrates both Christianity and the West. It denounces American patriotism and condemns wars that fight for freedom. It whitewashes Islamic terrorism, sometimes even exalting Islam. Hollywood's writers and producers often seem to rewrite history to suit their own political purposes. Much of this pattern is based on influence by Muslim Brotherhood front-groups allied with naïve, coerced, bullied, or anti-American Hollywood elites.

Of course, people who identify themselves as Muslim have the right to produce, write, or appear in films the same way everyone else does. We need to recognize, however, that the Global Jihad Movement, comprised of Islamic supremacists who aspire to replace the U.S. Constitution with shariah, is attempting to create an environment which gradually and incrementally inches toward their ultimate goals, even if the goals are not reached within their own lifetimes.

Pro-shariah advocacy is not simply a religious matter as the Muslim Brotherhood affiliates would have you believe. This is primarily a political movement cloaked in the language of religion (with some legitimate political aspects) and hiding behind U.S. Constitutional protections in order to achieve its liberty-crushing aspirations. Those who adhere to this totalitarian ideology seek preferential treatment and political domination. They use a range of tactics to achieve their supremacist utopia.

Nor are we in a War on Terror, as previously made clear. Though there's a military component, we are primarily in a War of Ideas against the Global Jihad Movement. The main current battle is one for information dominance.

Those who control the language, culture, and the information battlespace can better control the future and undermine their ideological enemies. The civilization jihadi tactics of lawsuits, infiltration, disinformation campaigns, coercion, and influence operations occur throughout every sphere of society. And, as this monograph has demonstrated, even Hollywood is not immune from Islamist influence.

"Documentaries" and whitewashed Hollywood films are created under the nefarious influence of Muslim Brotherhood groups and their allies who peddle lies, deception, and falsehoods to an unknowing public. These films are part of a broader campaign of disinformation and influence designed to confuse and mislead the public. Disinformation leads to bad decision-making, especially in the realm of national security. And that is exactly the goal of Islamic supremacist groups: to create a foundation of erroneous information, false premises and confusion so that the decision-makers of today and the leaders of tomorrow will make social, political, legal, academic and military decisions that betray their own self-interests and favor our enemies.

Hollywood constitutes a primary purveyor of social and political change. As one of society's most effective and perhaps overlooked change agents, Hollywood has been targeted for exploitation to aid America's ideological enemies. Eventually the false narratives become part of society's social fabric. The public and those in positions of power do not even realize they have been influenced. Indeed, this is the strategy that the Muslim Brotherhood outlined in its 1991 Explanatory Memorandum when it wrote of sabotaging the West from within by their hands and the hands of the believers.[463]

Tyrannical governments world-wide control their media, reporters, and press in order to suppress the free flow of information: both its dissemination and its receipt. Yet screen-writers, directors and film-producers, many of whom claim to be liberal, no longer fight for the classical liberal values of free speech, artistic license and critical thinking.

Information is power. Ignorance is *not* bliss. What you don't know *can* hurt you. Only by speaking the truth—even, and perhaps especially, in Hollywood—will America remain free.

DEBORAH WEISS, ESQ., is a Senior Fellow at the Center for Security Policy. She is an attorney, author, and public speaker specializing in free speech and terrorism-related issues, and is considered an expert on the Organization of Islamic Cooperation and CAIR.

Formerly, she was the Manhattan Director for the Forbes for President Campaign; Assistant Corporation Counsel in the Giuliani Administration, and a Counsel for the Committee on House Oversight in Congress. She is the author of a monograph titled, "The Organization of Islamic Cooperation's Jihad Against Free Speech"; the primary writer and researcher for the book: "Council on American Islamic Relations: Its use of Lawfare and Intimidation", and a contributing author to the book: "Saudi Arabia and the Global Islamic Terrorist Network."

Ms. Weiss is a regular contributor to FrontPage Magazine. Her articles have also been published in National Review Online, The Weekly Standard, The Washington Times, Human Events Online, and American Thinker. She speaks regularly throughout the United States and is a frequent guest on radio. Ms. Weiss is a survivor from the 9/11 attacks in New York City. A partial listing of her work can be found at: www.vigilancenow.org.

REFERENCES

[1] http://www.meforum.org/357/what-does-jihad-mean

[2] Warner, Bill, Sharia Law for Non-Muslims, (Center for the Study of Popular of Political Islam, 2010), p. 7.; See also S. Solomon & D. Alamaaqdisi, The Mosque Exposed, (ANM Press, 2006), p.50.

[3] Team B II, *Shariah the Threat to America*, (The Center for Security Policy, 2010), pp. 83-84.

[4] http://shariahthethreat.org/a-short-course-1-what-is-shariah/

[5] American Center for Law and Justice (ACLJ), Shari'ah Law: Radical Islam's Threat to the U.S. Constitution, p. 7.

[6] https://citizensagainstsharia.wordpress.com/tag/caliphate/; See also http://www.danielpipes.org/2798/what-do-the-terrorists-want-a-caliphate

[7] ACLJ, *Shari'ah Law*, pp. 8-9.

[8] S. Solomon, *The Mosque*, p.26.

[9] http://www.discoverthenetworks.org/viewSubCategory.asp?id=774

[10] https://www.youtube.com/watch?v=Ka4CFacEe1A

[11] ACLJ, *Shari'ah Law*, pp. 17-21.

[12] http://www.americanthinker.com/articles/2008/12/human_rights_vs_islamic_rights.html

[13] See http://www.churchisraelforum.com/dhimmi/; See also, Team B II, *Shariah the Threat*, p. 235; See also http://www.dhimmitude.org/d_history_dhimmitude.html (Dhimmitude is a state of second class citizenry, afforded to Jews and Christians if they agree to pay a poll tax known as the jizya, and subjugate themselves to Shariah. The dhimma contract permits People of the Book to live and worship within the confines of Shariah and are afforded temporary "peace" in exchange for this tax, which effectively constitutes ransom.)

[14] http://www.newenglishreview.org/blog_direct_link.cfm/blog_id/62135/A-Theology-Of-War

[15] ACLJ, *Shari'ah Law*, p. 9.

[16] See https://www.investigativeproject.org/documents/20-an-explanatory-memorandum-on-the-general.pdf

[17] https://fas.org/irp/world/para/mb.htm

[18] See generally https://www.investigativeproject.org/documents/20-an-explanatory-memorandum-on-the-general.pdf

[19] Team B II, "Shariah the Threat," p. 120.

[20] See generally https://www.investigativeproject.org/documents/20-an-explanatory-memorandum-on-the-general.pdf

[21] See generally https://www.investigativeproject.org/documents/20-an-explanatory-memorandum-on-the-general.pdf

[22] https://www.investigativeproject.org/documents/20-an-explanatory-memorandum-on-the-general.pdf, p. 18 of 18, (English).

[23] https://www.investigativeproject.org/documents/20-an-explanatory-memorandum-on-the-general.pdf, p. 7 of 18, (English).

[24] Da'wa literally means "call," "invitation" or "propaganda." ACLJ, *Shari'ah Law*, p 13.

25 http://www.rand.org/content/dam/rand/pubs/monographs/2009/
RAND_MG654.pdf, p. 2.

26 "If you know the enemy and know yourself, you need not fear the result of a hundred battles.
If you know yourself but not the enemy, for every victory gained you will also suffer a defeat.
If you know neither the enemy nor yourself, you will succumb in every battle." Tzu, Sun, *The
Art of War,* https://suntzusaid.com/artofwar.pdf, p. 11, para. 18.

27 https://southfront.org/terrorism-is-not-an-enemy-its-a-tactic/

28 http://www.wnd.com/2016/06/dhs-whistleblower-terrorism-is-not-the-enemy/

29 http://www.frontpagemag.com/fpm/264142/fifteen-years-after-911-living-910-world-
deborah-weiss

30 See, e.g, http://www.frontpagemag.com/fpm/261550/democrats-castigate-anti-muslim-
speech-proposed-deborah-weiss

31 See, e.g., Weiss, Deborah, The Organization of Islamic Cooperation's Jihad on Free Speech,
(The Center for Security Policy, 2015), pp. 24, 33-34, See, e.g, Council on American-Islamic
Relations: Its Use of Lawfare and Intimidation, (authored by Deborah Weiss, published
under the name of Citizens for National Security, "CFNS," 2013), p. 16.

32 Muslim Brotherhood front-groups often complain that programs, initiatives or legislation
designed to protect America from Islamic terrorism, is Islamophobic or bigoted. See, e.g.,
https://www.cair.com/press-center/press-releases/12876-california-muslim-groups-vote-
to-oppose-federal-cve-program.html . See also CFNS-Weiss, *Council on American-Islamic
Relations*, pp. 11-12, 17-19, and see generally pp. 45-88 for examples of CAIR's opposition to
national security training and law enforcement.

33 This applies especially to speech that properly identifies the enemy and speech that is
deemed to violate Islamic blasphemy laws.

34 http://variety.com/2016/biz/news/orlando-nightclub-shootings-donald-trump-hillary-
clinton-react-1201793724/

35 See e.g. http://www.out.com/entertainment/popnography/2014/04/17/10-queer-
producers-making-waves-hollywood

36 http://www.hollywoodreporter.com/news/orlando-gay-nightclub-shooting-world-901876

37 However, it's important to note that even when Obama Administration officials
acknowledged the terrorist nature of the act, their strategy to defeat ISIS in the war of ideas
was woefully insufficient, to say the least. In the case of the Orlando massacre, then-Attorney
General Loretta Lynch proclaimed that "our most effective response to terror is compassion
and love." http://www.mediaite.com/tv/loretta-lynch-our-most-effective-response-to-
terror-is-compassion-and-love/

38 https://www.education.com/reference/article/media-as-influence-socialization/;
http://www.123helpme.com/media-as-an-agent-in-socialization-view.asp?id=150259

39 http://www.hollywoodreporter.com/news/exodus-gods-kings-christian-bale-754781

40 CFNS-Weiss, Council on American-Islamic Relations, pp. 4-11.

41 CFNS-Weiss, Council on American-Islamic Relations, pp. 4-6.

42 https://www.investigativeproject.org/1854/doj-cairs-unindicted-co-conspirator-status-
legit

43 See, e.g., CFNS-Weiss, Council on American-Islamic Relations, pp.8-10.

44 http://www.discoverthenetworks.org/printgroupProfile.asp?grpid=6176;
http://www.nationalreview.com/article/393614/cair-terror-group-daniel-pipes

45 http://dailycaller.com/2014/11/15/united-arab-emirates-designates-two-american-muslim-groups-as-terrorist-orgs/; Also http://www.clarionproject.org/analysis/uae-doubles-down-designation-cair-terrorists#.

46 See generally CFNS-Weiss, *Council on American-Islamic Relations*, pp. 16-18.

47 http://humanevents.com/2015/08/08/islamist-influence-in-hollywood/; See also https://www.facebook.com/pg/1.nihadawad/about/?ref=page_internal ; See also http://www.discoverthenetworks.org/individualProfile.asp?indid=755

48 http://www.investigativeproject.org/2100/cairs-hollywood-crusade

49 https://www.investigativeproject.org/223/cairs-awad-in-support-of-the-hamas-movement; See also http://www.discoverthenetworks.org/printgroupProfile.asp?grpid=6176

50 http://www.investigativeproject.org/2100/cairs-hollywood-crusade

51 https://www.investigativeproject.org/2100/cairs-hollywood-crusade; See also http://www.meforum.org/26/muslims-on-the-silver-screen

52 http://www.meforum.org/26/muslims-on-the-silver-screen; See also CFNS-Weiss, *Council on American-Islamic Relations*, p. 125.

53 http://www.meforum.org/26/muslims-on-the-silver-screen; See also CFNS-Weiss, *Council on American-Islamic Relations*, p. 123.

54 https://www.investigativeproject.org/2100/cairs-hollywood-crusade

55 http://www.meforum.org/26/muslims-on-the-silver-screen; See also https://www.cair.com/about-us/cair-who-we-are.html#Defamation2

56 http://www.imdb.com/title/tt0116253/alternateversions

57 http://www.imdb.com/title/tt0116253/alternateversions

58 http://www.imdb.com/title/tt0116253/alternateversions

59 See, http://www.imdb.com/title/tt0116253/alternateversions

60 http://www.meforum.org/26/muslims-on-the-silver-screen; http://www.cair.com/action-alerts/131-rules-of-engagement-stereotypes-muslims.html

61 http://www.imdb.com/title/tt0160797/plotsummary

62 http://www.cair.com/action-alerts/131-rules-of-engagement-stereotypes-muslims.html

63 http://www.cair.com/action-alerts/131-rules-of-engagement-stereotypes-muslims.html

64 See https://www.wrmea.org/2000-june/rules-of-engagement-a-highwater-mark-in-hollywood-hate-mongering-with-u.s.-military-cooperation.html

65 http://www.countercontempt.com/archives/1893; See also CFNS-Weiss, *Council on American-Islamic Relations*, pp. 127-128.

66 http://www.countercontempt.com/archives/1893

67 At the time, the OIC claimed to represent 1.3 billion Muslims. http://www.countercontempt.com/archives/1893 It has since changed its name to the Organization of Islamic Cooperation and expanded its membership to 56 Muslim majority countries plus the Palestinian Authority, claiming to represent 1.5 billion Muslims worldwide. See Weiss, *The Organization of Islamic Cooperation*, p. 13.

68 http://www.cnsnews.com/news/article/islamic-group-expresses-concern-over-24-terror-storyline; See also http://www.militantislammonitor.org/article/id/376; See also

http://www.fox.com/article/fox-orders-24-legacy; See also CFNS-Weiss, *Council on American-Islamic Relations*, pp. 122-123.

[69] http://www.ew.com/article/2014/03/21/abc-family-muslims-alice-in-arabia

[70] http://www.hollywoodreporter.com/news/alice-arabia-writer-media-mob-691453

[71] http://www.adc.org/2014/03/breaking-disney-and-abc-family-drop-alice-in-arabia/

[72] http://www.adc.org/2014/03/breaking-disney-and-abc-family-drop-alice-in-arabia/

[73] See generally http://www.discoverthenetworks.org/viewSubCategory.asp?id=774

[74] http://www.who.int/mediacentre/factsheets/fs241/en/

[75] Spencer, Robert, The Politically Incorrect Guide to Islam (and the Crusades), (Regnery Publishing, 2005), p. 69.

[76] See, e.g., http://www.girlsnotbrides.org/child-marriage/iran/

[77] See Spencer, Robert, *The Politically Incorrect Guide to Islam,* p. 69. See also https://www.jihadwatch.org/2013/05/robert-spencer-the-silent-tragedy-of-child-marriage

[78] http://news.nationalgeographic.com/news/2002/02/0212_020212_honorkilling.html

[79] https://www.theatlantic.com/politics/archive/2015/04/honor-killings-in-america/391760/; See generally: http://www.meforum.org/2646/worldwide-trends-in-honor-killings; See also http://pantheon.hrw.org/legacy/press/2001/04/un_oral12_0405.htm; See also https://www.youtube.com/watch?v=KXFs4mrEpEc

[80] http://www.honordiaries.com/about-the-filmmakers/

[81] See generally, http://www.honordiaries.com/about-the-film/

[82] http://www.frontpagemag.com/point/222439/cair-attacks-honor-diaries-movie-about-abuse-women-daniel-greenfield

[83] http://www.thenewamerican.com/culture/faith-and-morals/item/17996-islamist-front-group-cair-moves-against-honor-diaries-film

[84] http://www.csmonitor.com/USA/USA-Update/2015/0414/Colleges-wrestle-with-screening-American-Sniper

[85] http://www.thenewamerican.com/culture/faith-and-morals/item/17996-islamist-front-group-cair-moves-against-honor-diaries-film; Also http://www.csmonitor.com/USA/USA-Update/2015/0414/Colleges-wrestle-with-screening-American-Sniper

[86] http://www.csmonitor.com/USA/USA-Update/2015/0414/Colleges-wrestle-with-screening-American-Sniper

[87] "The Third Jihad" was produced by Raphael Shore, Founder of the Clarion Fund, 2008.

[88] http://www.thethirdjihad.com/about_new.php

[89] http://www.frontpagemag.com/fpm/121033/nypd-caves-cair-arnold-ahlert

[90] http://www.frontpagemag.com/fpm/225420/911-museum-refuses-censor-al-qaeda-film-deborah-weiss

[91] See e.g., http://www.cair.com/press-center/press-releases/12415-cair-asks-abc-family-channel-for-meeting-on-alice-in-arabia-stereotypes.html

[92] See e.g., http://www.cair.com/press-center/press-releases/12415-cair-asks-abc-family-channel-for-meeting-on-alice-in-arabia-stereotypes.html

[93] Compare with… http://articles.latimes.com/2011/dec/12/opinion/la-oe-turley-blasphemy-20111210 The Organization of Islamic Cooperation pushes resolutions ostensibly to stop

"incitement to violence," but upon further examination, the resolutions urge to curtail any speech that "defames Islam" tantamount to blasphemy laws. For further discussion on this issue in regard to the OIC, see Weiss, Deborah, *The Organization of Islamic Cooperation's Jihad on Free Speech.*

94 https://www.worldwatchmonitor.org/2016/08/in-new-report-on-religious-freedom-us-government-turns-its-attention-to-blasphemy-laws/

95 http://humanevents.com/2015/08/08/islamist-influence-in-hollywood/

96 http://www.nationalreview.com/article/313257/history-mpac-andrew-c-mccarthy; See http://www.discoverthenetworks.org/printgroupProfile.asp?grpid=6177; Also http://www.clarionproject.org/analysis/muslim-public-affairs-council-mpac

97 http://www.mpac.org/policy-analysis/accepting-our-identities-the-patriotic-way.php

98 https://www.mpac.org/safespaces/

99 http://www.mpac.org/programs.php

100 http://www.mpac.org/programs/government-relations.php

101 http://www.nationalreview.com/article/313257/history-mpac-andrew-c-mccarthy; Note that Hizballah is a State-designated Foreign Terrorist Organization.

102 http://www.clarionproject.org/analysis/muslim-public-affairs-council-mpac; http://www.frontpagemag.com/fpm/168402/exposed-islamist-group-scrambles-ryan-mauro

103 See generally http://www.discoverthenetworks.org/printgroupProfile.asp?grpid=6386; See also http://www.discoverthenetworks.org/individualProfile.asp?indid=1368; For a general discussion on offensive vs. defensive jihad see, http://www.jpost.com/Opinion/Op-Ed-Contributors/Defensive-or-offensive-Jihad-History-exegesis-vs-contemporary-propagation-343597

104 Al-Maryati was formerly the head of MPAC prior to working as an appointee to the Obama Administration. http://www.debbieschlussel.com/6259/jihad-on-24%C2%A0-fox-kiefer-sutherland-repent-to-radical-islam/ ; Also http://www.investigativeproject.org/profile/114/salam-al-marayati

105 http://freebeacon.com/national-security/state-stands-by-its-man/

106 See http://www.debbieschlussel.com/6259/jihad-on-24%C2%A0-fox-kiefer-sutherland-repent-to-radical-islam/; see also http://freebeacon.com/politics/anti-israel-advocate-reps-u-s-at-rights-conference/

107 http://www.mpac.org/programs/hollywood-bureau.php

108 http://www.mpac.org/programs/hollywood-bureau.php

109 http://www.mpac.org/programs/hollywood-bureau.php

110 http://www.investigativeproject.org/2100/cairs-hollywood-crusade

111 http://www.mpac.org/programs/hollywood-bureau.php

112 See generally http://summits.mpac.org/?mc_cid=cfe0955885&mc_eid=920f73b6a1

113 https://www.mpac.org/blog/illuminating-muslim-narratives-at-the-sundance-film-festival.php?mc_cid=cfe0955885&mc_eid=920f73b6a1

114 http://www.sundance.org/about/us

115 https://www.mpac.org/blog/illuminating-muslim-narratives-at-the-sundance-film-festival.php?mc_cid=cfe0955885&mc_eid=920f73b6a1

116 http://www.mpac.org/programs/hollywood-bureau.php

117 http://media-
awards.mpac.org/?mc_cid=58e9b23cb9&mc_eid=2887361116&mc_cid=cfe0955885&mc_
eid=920f73b6a1

118 http://www.investigativeproject.org/2100/cairs-hollywood-crusade

119 http://www.mpac.org/programs/hollywood-bureau.php

120 See https://www.mpac.org/blog/illuminating-muslim-narratives-at-the-sundance-film-
festival.php?mc_cid=cfe0955885&mc_eid=920f73b6a1

121 See https://www.investigativeproject.org/2100/cairs-hollywood-crusade#

122 http://www.goldenglobes.com/film/paradise-now

123 http://www.imdb.com/title/tt0445620/awards

124 See http://www.nysun.com/foreign/spielbergs-munich-is-criticized/24301/

125 http://www.imdb.com/title/tt0408306/awards

126 See http://www.washingtonpost.com/wp-
dyn/content/article/2006/03/02/AR2006030201209.html

127 http://www.imdb.com/title/tt0365737/awards

128 http://www.promotingpeace.org/2010/3/unaoc.html

129 https://berkleycenter.georgetown.edu/programs/alliance-of-civilizations-media-fund

130 http://www.cair.com/press-center/cair-in-the-news/10443-hollywood-backs-fund-for-
films-that-combat-stereotypes.html

131 http://www.cnn.com/WORLD/meast/9902/07/king.hussein.obit/

132 http://www.promotingpeace.org/2010/3/unaoc.html

133 http://www.unaoc.org/images/aoc%20forum%20report%20madrid%20
complete.pdf

134 http://www.unaoc.org/images/aoc%20forum%20report%20madrid%20
complete.pdf

135http://www.cair.com/press-center/cair-in-the-news/10443-hollywood-backs-fund-for-
films-that-combat-stereotypes.html

136 http://www.unaoc.org/images/aoc%20forum%20report%20madrid%20
complete.pdf

137 https://berkleycenter.georgetown.edu/programs/alliance-of-civilizations-media-fund

138 https://www.upf.tv/most-resource-2/

139 https://www.upf.tv/about-upf/

140 https://www.upf.tv/about-upf/

141 See, e.g., https://www.upf.tv/wp-content/uploads/sites/196/2016/06/UPF-990-PD-2015-
.pdf

142 See http://990s.foundationcenter.org/990_pdf_archive/770/770519274/
770519274_201412_990.pdf

143 https://www.upf.tv/about-upf/

144 https://www.upf.tv/about-upf/

145 See https://www.upf.tv/films/

146 https://www.upf.tv/about-upf/

147 https://www.upf.tv/about-upf/

148 https://www.upf.tv/about-upf/

149 https://www.upf.tv/about-upf/staff/

150 https://www.upf.tv/about-upf/staff/

151 See http://www.connecting-cultures.net/About%20Us/team.htm

152 Secretary Albright asserted that she initiated the Iftar dinner at the suggestion of Alex Kronemer and others, and she intended the event to occur annually. At 2009 address at Georgetown University, she mentioned this prior to a viewing of UPF's film, "Inside Islam: What a Billion Muslims Really Think." https://www.upf.tv/wp-content/uploads/sites/196/2014/05/inside-islam-albright-keynote-premier.pdf, p.3.

153 https://www.upf.tv/about-upf/; https://www.upf.tv/about-upf/staff/

154 http://www.michaelwolfeauthor.com/bio.htm

155 See https://www.upf.tv/about-upf/staff/; See also http://www.michaelwolfeauthor.com/bio.htm

156 It should be noted that many of these universities receive large donations of Saudi money. See, e.g., http://abcnews.go.com/International/story?id=1402008; See also http://www.campus-watch.org/article/id/15699; See also http://nationalinterest.org/commentary/saudi-money-shaping-us-research-8083

157 https://www.upf.tv/about-upf/staff/

158 See https://www.upf.tv/teachers/

159 https://www.upf.tv/outreach/

160 https://www.upf.tv/outreach/

161 Weiss, Deborah, The Organization of Islamic Cooperation's Jihad on Free Speech, p. 16.

162 See http://www.citizentimes.eu/2013/06/13/if-you-criticize-islam-you-will-suffer-consequences/

163 America's First Amendment's free speech clause is unique and includes the freedom to speak all true statements of fact as well as opinions, even if offensive. Contrast this with European countries that ostensibly have freedom of speech but which exclude various forms of "hate speech" from legal protection. See generally, http://www.legal-project.org/issues/european-hate-speech-laws The Organization of Islamic Cooperation insists that it believes in "free speech" but is quick to follow up by asserting that "blasphemous speech" is not included in its definition of free speech. Weiss, Deborah, *The Organization of Islamic Cooperation's Jihad on Free Speech*, p. 16.

164 https://www.upf.tv/outreach/

165 See Weiss, Deborah, The Organization of Islamic Cooperation's Jihad on Free Speech, pp. 33-34.

166 See, e.g., http://www.frontpagemag.com/fpm/221407/holocaust-heroine-motivated-islam-deborah-weiss; See also http://www.frontpagemag.com/fpm/98787/prince-lies-daniel-greenfield

167 https://www.upf.tv/outreach/

168 See https://www.upf.tv/outreach/

169 https://www.upf.tv/outreach/

170 See also Chapter 7, "The Hollywood-Islamist Alliance," subsection on "Hollywood's First Iftar Dinner" for more information on MOST's role in this event.

171 https://www.upf.tv/most-resource-2/

172 See https://www.upf.tv/most-resource-2/

173 https://www.upf.tv/most-resource-2/

[174] https://www.upf.tv/most-resource-2/

[175] See Chapter 5 of this monograph for more information on the Alliance of Civilizations Media Fund.

[176] See, e.g., Program, "World Premiere, Unity Productions Foundation presents Enemy of the Reich: the Noor Inayat Khan Story," Warner Theater, Washington, DC, February 15, 2014.

[177] https://www.investigativeproject.org/documents/20-an-explanatory-memorandum-on-the-general.pdf, p. 18 of 18, (English).

[178] See http://www.isna.net/speaker-biographies.html

[179] http://www.muslimlinkpaper.com/national-news/4005-countering-islamophobia-topic-at-isna

[180] See https://www.upf.tv/isna53/

[181] https://www.investigativeproject.org/1854/doj-cairs-unindicted-co-conspirator-status-legit

[182] https://www.upf.tv/islamophobia/

[183] http://www.frontpagemag.com/fpm/256978/tweeting-islamist-propaganda-deborah-weiss

[184] https://sfs.georgetown.edu/faculty-bio/john-esposito/#_ga=1.60245165.1688235712.1492364917

[185] http://bridge.georgetown.edu/team/

[186] http://edition.cnn.com/2001/US/10/11/rec.giuliani.prince/ As a side note, Prince Alwaleed bin Talal is the second largest shareholder in 21st Century Fox which the parent company of Foxnews. Only the Murdoch family, with whom the Prince is good friends, owns more shares. This has, in some instances influenced Fox's reporting on Islam-related news. http://www.aim.org/aim-column/scandal-rocks-fox-news-over-saudi-terror-link/

[187] Prince Mohammad bin Salmon implemented this unprecedented anti-corruption initiative. The allegations are awaiting corroboration and it is yet to be determined whether they are true or merely part of a move on bin Salmon's part to consolidate power. See https://www.reuters.com/article/us-saudi-arrests/future-saudi-king-tightens-grip-on-power-with-arrests-including-prince-alwaleed-idUSKBN1D506P; http://time.com/5012396/saudi-arabia-prince-alwaleed-bin-talal-arrested/; https://www.nytimes.com/2017/11/04/world/middleeast/saudi-arabia-waleed-bin-talal.html;

[188] For example, the Washington, DC premiere of UPF's film "Enemy of the Reich" on February 15, 2014 cited in the program a thank you to several Muslim Brotherhood front-groups including the Muslim Students Association, and the Islamic Society of North America (an unindicted co-conspirator in the Holy Land Foundation Trial), and the International Institute of Islamic Thought, as well as the El-Hibri Foundation (which though not listed in the Muslim Brotherhood's 1991 Explanatory Memorandum as an affiliate, is still like minded with questionable ties discussed further under "Muhammad: Legacy of a Prophet).

[189] http://www.enemyofthereich.com/premieres/

[190] Program, "*World Premiere, Unity Productions Foundation presents Enemy of the Reich: the Noor Inayat Khan Story,*" Warner Theater, Washington, DC, February 15, 2014. It should be noted that both Rashad Hussein and Suhail Khan are Islamic supremacists with numerous nefarious ties.

[191] There were questionable assertions made by each of the speakers. However, it is not the purpose of this monograph to dissect each presentation, but rather to demonstrate how UPF as a whole is manufacturing false narratives and inserting them into the public sphere

with the aid of government agencies, the faith community, film producers and television stations.

192 http://www.pbs.org/program/enemy-reich/

193 http://www.frontpagemag.com/fpm/221407/holocaust-heroine-motivated-islam-deborah-weiss

194 http://www.pbs.org/program/enemy-reich/

195 Unfortunately, Khan had kept notebooks memorializing her wireless messages to Britain. The notebooks were found and the SD continued to send Britain wireless messages using Khan's code name. http://www.frontpagemag.com/fpm/221407/holocaust-heroine-motivated-islam-deborah-weiss

196 http://www.frontpagemag.com/fpm/221407/holocaust-heroine-motivated-islam-deborah-weiss

197 http://www.frontpagemag.com/fpm/221407/holocaust-heroine-motivated-islam-deborah-weiss

198 http://www.frontpagemag.com/fpm/221407/holocaust-heroine-motivated-islam-deborah-weiss

199 http://www.frontpagemag.com/fpm/221407/holocaust-heroine-motivated-islam-deborah-weiss

200 http://www.frontpagemag.com/fpm/221407/holocaust-heroine-motivated-islam-deborah-weiss

201 http://www.frontpagemag.com/fpm/221407/holocaust-heroine-motivated-islam-deborah-weiss; Kronemer conveniently omits the special relationship that the Grand Mufti of Jerusalem had with Hitler and his participation in Nazi atrocities, as well as his assistance informing a Nazi Unit for Muslims and encouraging them to join. Kronemer ignores entirely the Waffen SS unit comprised entirely of Bosnian Muslims. http://www.discoverthenetworks.org/individualProfile.asp?indid=2150 He also disregards Hitler's alliance with the Muslim Brotherhood. http://www.discoverthenetworks.org/viewSubCategory.asp?id=764 It appears that the basis for these Muslim-Nazi relationships is their shared Jew hatred. For an in depth discussion on this topic, see generally, Bostom, Andrew G., *"The Mufti's Islamic Jew Hatred"*(Bravura Books, 2013).

202 http://www.frontpagemag.com/fpm/221407/holocaust-heroine-motivated-islam-deborah-weiss

203 http://www.frontpagemag.com/fpm/221407/holocaust-heroine-motivated-islam-deborah-weiss

204 http://www.frontpagemag.com/fpm/221407/holocaust-heroine-motivated-islam-deborah-weiss

205 http://www.frontpagemag.com/fpm/221407/holocaust-heroine-motivated-islam-deborah-weiss

206 http://www.frontpagemag.com/fpm/221407/holocaust-heroine-motivated-islam-deborah-weiss

207 http://www.frontpagemag.com/fpm/221407/holocaust-heroine-motivated-islam-deborah-weiss

208 http://www.frontpagemag.com/fpm/221407/holocaust-heroine-motivated-islam-deborah-weiss

209 http://www.frontpagemag.com/fpm/221407/holocaust-heroine-motivated-islam-deborah-weiss

210 https://www.upf.tv/films/muhammad-legacy-of-a-prophet/

211 https://www.upf.tv/films/muhammad-legacy-of-a-prophet/

212 https://www.upf.tv/films/muhammad-legacy-of-a-prophet/

213 https://www.upf.tv/films/muhammad-legacy-of-a-prophet/

214 Robert Spencer, "The Politically Incorrect Guide to Islam and the Crusades," (Regnery Publishing, Inc., 2005), p. 107.

215 See generally http://www.dhimmitude.org/d_history_dhimmitude.html

216 http://www.pewresearch.org/fact-tank/2016/01/06/a-new-estimate-of-the-u-s-muslim-population/

217 https://www.upf.tv/films/muhammad-legacy-of-a-prophet/

218 http://www.fjponline.com/

219 The Muslim Brotherhood's version of "freedom" means freedom from "man-made law." In other words, freedom means Shariah. Justice means justice as meted out under Shariah and law means Islamic law. See https://www.centerforsecuritypolicy.org/2015/12/22/muslim-brotherhoods-uscmo-launches-2016-political-campaign/

220 http://www.freep.com/story/news/local/michigan/wayne/2015/06/05/imam-qazwini-resigns-dearborn-mosque/28581129/

221 http://www.npr.org/2015/09/14/440215976/journalist-says-the-drone-strike-that-killed-awlaki-did-not-silence-him

222 http://www.islamproject.org/muhammad/muhammad.htm

223 http://www.frontpagemag.com/fpm/106910/defense-contractors-islam-daniel-greenfield

224 http://www.investigativeproject.org/profile/187/azizah-y-al-hibri; http://karamah.org/about/what-we-do

225 The author attended this movie screening and discussion group personally, and was one of two non-hijabbed women in attendance.

226 The author attended an interfaith panel that El-Hibri was on in Washington, DC, where she told a story about a young female relative of hers who didn't want to wear her hijab outside because she was "afraid" that people would make negative comments about her. El-Hibri followed up by stating that this relative shouldn't have to live in a country where she's afraid, as though the relative's subjective fear is an objective statement about America's stance on Muslims.

227 http://www.investigativeproject.org/profile/187/azizah-y-al-hibri

228 http://www.arabnews.com/node/296493

229 http://www.investigativeproject.org/profile/187/azizah-y-al-hibri

230 http://www.frontpagemag.com/fpm/106910/defense-contractors-islam-daniel-greenfield

231 http://www.frontpagemag.com/fpm/106910/defense-contractors-islam-daniel-greenfield

232 http://www.pif.org.pk/safi-qureshey/

233 http://www.frontpagemag.com/fpm/98787/prince-lies-daniel-greenfield

234 https://www.upf.tv/films/muhammad-legacy-of-a-prophet/

235 https://www.gatestoneinstitute.org/5211/pbs-islam

236 https://www.gatestoneinstitute.org/5211/pbs-islam

237 http://sparkmedia.org/about/get-involved/

238 http://www.dukemediafoundation.org/about.html

239 http://princeamongslaves.org/about/film

240 http://princeamongslaves.org/about/film

241 http://www.frontpagemag.com/fpm/98787/prince-lies-daniel-greenfield

242 See http://princeamongslaves.org/about/film

243 http://www.frontpagemag.com/fpm/98787/prince-lies-daniel-greenfield

244 http://www.frontpagemag.com/fpm/98787/prince-lies-daniel-greenfield

245 http://www.frontpagemag.com/fpm/251099/revisionist-muslim-history-america-daniel-greenfield; http://www.frontpagemag.com/fpm/98787/prince-lies-daniel-greenfield

246 http://www.frontpagemag.com/fpm/251099/revisionist-muslim-history-america-daniel-greenfield; http://www.frontpagemag.com/fpm/98787/prince-lies-daniel-greenfield

247 http://www.frontpagemag.com/fpm/98787/prince-lies-daniel-greenfield

248 http://www.answering-islam.org/Bailey/real_slave_master.html

249 https://www.firstthings.com/web-exclusives/2008/02/slavery-christianity-and-islam

250 https://www.thoughtco.com/the-role-of-islam-in-african-slavery-44532

251 http://www.discoverthenetworks.org/viewSubCategory.asp?id=785

252 http://www.discoverthenetworks.org/viewSubCategory.asp?id=785

253 http://www.discoverthenetworks.org/viewSubCategory.asp?id=785

254 http://www.discoverthenetworks.org/viewSubCategory.asp?id=785

255 https://www.youtube.com/watch?v=G51lJ-0L2eA

256 See https://www.upf.tv/outreach/; See also http://princeamongslaves.org/about/film

257 http://www.connecting-cultures.net/new/people.html

258 http://www.connecting-cultures.net/new/people.html

259 http://www.connecting-cultures.net/new/people.html

260 http://www.connecting-cultures.net/new/about.html

261 http://www.connecting-cultures.net/new/clients.html

262 http://www.connecting-cultures.net/new/index.html

263 See http://www.connecting-cultures.net/new/about.html

264 https://counterjihadreport.com/tag/unity-productions-foundation-upf/ click link to video, *"The First 3 to 5 seconds: Understanding Arab and Muslim Americans"*; See also https://www.justice.gov/crs/first-three-five-seconds (NOTE: this link originally showed a short clip of the training video, but the URL has since been erased).

265 https://www.youtube.com/watch?v=HOQt_mP6Pgg

266 http://islamicscholarshipfund.org/mission/

267 http://islamicscholarshipfund.org/mission/

268 http://islamicscholarshipfund.org/mission/

269 http://www.pewresearch.org/fact-tank/2016/01/06/a-new-estimate-of-the-u-s-muslim-population/

270 Interestingly, Georgetown University sends out emails and posts events with advertisements for ISF. See, e.g., http://us9.campaign-archive1.com/?u=bba56a36303778d55a96e4a2b&id=29f9cb9077&e=81e0e4b738

271 http://islamicscholarshipfund.org/film-grants/

272 See http://islamicscholarshipfund.org/internships/

273 ISF partners with Islamic Centers and mosques to offer joint scholarships. See, e.g., http://islamicscholarshipfund.org/ISF-MCA-Scholarship/ See also https://islamicscholarshipfund.org/scholarships/

274 https://www.investigativeproject.org/documents/misc/20.pdf, pp.10-11 within the text.

275 In that vein, ISF scholarships do not support those who major in healthcare, economics, agriculture or psychology. http://islamicscholarshipfund.org/scholarships/

276 See http://islamicscholarshipfund.org/isf-supported-fields/

277 See http://islamicscholarshipfund.org/financial-resources/

278 See http://islamicscholarshipfund.org/scholarships/

279 https://islamicscholarshipfund.org/board-of-directors/

280 http://www.adl.org/israel-international/anti-israel-activity/c/students-justice-palestine.html#.VW4H_6JFB2Y

281 https://www.investigativeproject.org/documents/misc/31.pdf , p.18 of 18 within the text.

282 http://www.payvand.com/news/08/jul/1201.html

283 http://www.payvand.com/news/08/jul/1201.html

284 See http://www.cair.com/press-center/cair-in-the-news/5636-cair-muslim-arab-actors-seek-roles-that-combat-stereotypes.html; See also http://www.cnsnews.com/news/article/islamic-group-expresses-concern-over-24-terror-storyline and http://www.freerepublic.com/focus/f-news/1322728/posts and http://www.payvand.com/news/08/jul/1201.html

285 http://www.payvand.com/news/08/jul/1201.html

286 Participant Media was a founding partner of the Alliance of Organizations' Media Fund. For more information, see Chapter 5 of this monograph.

287 http://www.payvand.com/news/08/jul/1201.html

288 http://www.payvand.com/news/08/jul/1201.html

289 http://www.payvand.com/news/08/jul/1201.html

290 http://www.payvand.com/news/08/jul/1201.html

291 Dalia Mogahed regularly defends and supports Muslim Brotherhood front groups such as CAIR and ISNA. http://www.investigativeproject.org/1904/dalia-mogahed-a-muslim-george-gallup-or-islamist

292 CAIR sought a meeting with Fox producers after the premiere of "24" aired, portraying a Muslim family as a terrorist sleeper cell. http://www.freerepublic.com/focus/f-news/1322728/posts

293 See http://www.thenational.ae/arts-culture/film/operation-stereotype#page3

294 See http://www.mostresource.org/events/rewriting-the-divide-hollywood-and-the-muslim-world/

295 For more information, See Chapter 6, heading on Muslims on Screen and Television (MOST).

296 See, e.g., http://www.thenational.ae/arts-culture/film/operation-stereotype#page4 See also

297 See http://familyhistorydaily.com/personal-genealogy-stories/10-famous-immigrants-changed-names/

298 http://www.thenational.ae/arts-culture/film/operation-stereotype#page3

299 http://www.imdb.com/title/tt0371746/fullcredits/

300 http://www.imdb.com/title/tt0960144/fullcredits/

301 http://www.imdb.com/list/ls004407702/

302 http://www.patheos.com/blogs/deaconsbench/2015/07/rip-omar-sharif-catholic-who-became-a-muslim/

303 See, e.g., http://themuslimsarecoming.com/

304 https://www.youtube.com/watch?v=vln9D81eO60

305 https://www.youtube.com/watch?v=vln9D81eO60

306 https://www.youtube.com/watch?v=vln9D81eO60

307 http://www.imdb.com/name/nm0000255/awards

308 http://www.discoverthenetworks.org/individualProfile.asp?indid=2679

309 http://www.discoverthenetworks.org/viewSubCategory.asp?id=2337

310 http://www.discoverthenetworks.org/individualProfile.asp?indid=2679

311 http://www.discoverthenetworks.org/viewSubCategory.asp?id=2337

312 http://michaelmoore.com/WeAreAllMuslim/

313 See Michael Moore's website: http://michaelmoore.com/holy-crap

314 http://michaelmoore.com/WeAreAllMuslim/

315 http://michaelmoore.com/WeAreAllMuslim/

316 http://michaelmoore.com/WeAreAllMuslim/

317 See http://humanevents.com/2009/02/27/hollywood-mia-on-abuse-in-islam/

318 http://www.investigativeproject.org/2100/cairs-hollywood-crusade For more information on MPAC's influence in Hollywood, see chapter 3 of this monograph.

319 http://www.worldreligionnews.com/religion-news/buddhism/richard-geres-path-to-buddhism

320 See https://www.youtube.com/watch?v=a1nwIVGuQRg

321 See http://news.bbc.co.uk/1/hi/in_depth/uk/2000/newsmakers/2591237.stm

322 http://hollywoodhater.blogspot.com/2005/01/richard-gere-palestinian-political.html

323 See e.g., http://www.jewishworldreview.com/0105/borowitz_gere.php3

324 http://www.hollywoodreporter.com/news/richard-gere-open-film-counter-378557

325 http://www.chicagotribune.com/news/opinion/editorials/ct-benghazi-hillary-clinton-obama-rhodes-edit-0629-jm-20160628-story.html Within one day of the attack, it was well established that the events at Benghazi constituted a planned terrorist attack by an Al-Qaeda affiliate and were not a spontaneous uprising. https://www.usatoday.com/story/news/world/2015/05/18/benghazi-attack-intelligence-documents/27543563/

326 http://www.washingtontimes.com/news/2015/mar/19/sean-penn-thanks-george-bush-dick-cheney-for-inven/

327 See http://www.breitbart.com/big-hollywood/2014/09/30/rosie-o-donnell-penalizing-nfl-player-for-muslim-prayer-propels-us-to-war/

328 http://abcnews.go.com/International/story?id=83179&page=1

329 http://www.rollingstone.com/music/features/yusuf-islams-golden-years-cat-stevens-on-islam-and-his-return-to-music-20150113

330 http://majicat.com/yusufislam/aramco.html

331 See, e.g., http://www.brondesburycollege.co.uk/the-school/founders-message/ ; See, e.g., http://www.islamiaschools.com/the-school/founders-message/

332 http://nypost.com/2014/12/11/questions-remain-over-cat-stevens-connections-to-radical-muslims/ See also http://abcnews.go.com/International/story?id=83179&page=1

333 https://www.youtube.com/watch?v=1YVoChSTlKo

334 http://www.rollingstone.com/music/news/cat-stevens-breaks-his-silence-20000621 Note: In this interview, he claims that he never said he supported the death of Salmon Rushdie for blasphemy, and that he was merely explaining the Islamic doctrinal law. In other places, he claimed he was merely joking. Both of those are belied by the actual conversation seen here: https://www.youtube.com/watch?v=2-wjxwpvqps

335 See https://www.youtube.com/watch?v=2-wjxwpvqps

336 http://www.debbieschlussel.com/5187/hollywood-gushes-over-hamas-money-mule-rushdie-fatwah-supporter-cat-stevens/; See also http://nypost.com/2014/12/11/questions-remain-over-cat-stevens-connections-to-radical-muslims/ (Yusuf was allowed into the U.S. without incident).

337 See e.g. https://www.youtube.com/watch?v=2-wjxwpvqps

338 http://www.ocregister.com/articles/hollywood-725418-stevens-cat.html

339 http://www.beacontheatre.com/events/2016/september/yusuf-islam.html

340 http://hollywoodpantages.com/showinfo.php?id=90; See also http://www.smallkindness.org.uk/projects

341 http://archive.frontpagemag.com/readArticle.aspx?ARTID=34970

342 See http://www.oscars.org/education-grants/grants Yet, as indicated by the mission of the Academy's Grant program, the Academy is additionally committed to "diversity" as defined by the political left in a way that is divorced from anything to do with technical or artistic diversity.

343 See, e.g., http://www.cnn.com/2017/02/27/politics/oscars-politics/

344 See the Executive Order as issued at the time: https://www.whitehouse.gov/the-press-office/2017/01/27/executive-order-protecting-nation-foreign-terrorist-entry-united-states and the subsequent Executive Order: https://www.whitehouse.gov/the-press-office/2017/03/06/executive-order-protecting-nation-foreign-terrorist-entry-united-states

345 https://aclj.org/national-security/what-president-trumps-executive-order-on-immigration-and-refugees-does-and-does-not-do

346 http://www.cnn.com/2017/02/27/politics/oscars-politics/

347 http://www.breitbart.com/big-government/2017/02/27/exclusive-president-trump-oscar-fail-focused-hard-politics-not-get-basics-right/; See also http://www.hollywoodreporter.com/news/warren-beatty-faye-dunaway-stage-bonnie-clyde-reunion-oscars-2017-980193

348 http://ew.com/awards/2017/02/26/oscars-2017-white-helmets-doc-short/

349 http://www.theblaze.com/myvoice/entertainment/the-quran-verse-in-the-oscars/

350 http://www.frontpagemag.com/fpm/265946/asghar-farhadi-hollywood-hero-bruce-bawer

351 See generally
https://web.archive.org/web/20061211005211/http://www.caen.iufm.fr/colloque_iarte
m/pdf/knudsen.pdf

352 See, e.g., https://pjmedia.com/news-and-politics/2016/06/12/cair-on-orlando-attack-
homophobia-islamophobia-are-interconnected-systems-of-oppression/

353 http://www.redstate.com/bradslager/2017/02/26/hollywood-agency-cancels-oscar-
party-stages-immigration-rally/; See also
http://www.frontpagemag.com/fpm/265946/asghar-farhadi-hollywood-hero-bruce-
bawer

354 https://www.nytimes.com/2017/01/29/movies/trump-immigration-oscars-iranian-
director-asghar-farhadi.html?_r=0; See also
http://www.redstate.com/bradslager/2017/02/26/hollywood-agency-cancels-oscar-
party-stages-immigration-rally/

355 See http://www.redstate.com/bradslager/2017/02/26/hollywood-agency-cancels-oscar-
party-stages-immigration-rally/

356 http://www.latimes.com/entertainment/movies/la-et-mn-oscars-trump-ban-iran-asghar-
farhadi-salesman-20170128-story.html

357 http://www.avclub.com/article/asghar-farhadi-calls-empathy-oscars-acceptance-sta-
251095

358 http://www.redstate.com/bradslager/2017/02/26/hollywood-agency-cancels-oscar-
party-stages-immigration-rally/

359 http://www.redstate.com/bradslager/2017/02/26/hollywood-agency-cancels-oscar-
party-stages-immigration-rally/

360 http://www.redstate.com/bradslager/2017/02/26/hollywood-agency-cancels-oscar-
party-stages-immigration-rally/
http://www.latimes.com/entertainment/movies/la-et-mn-oscars-2017-uta-immigration-
rally-20170224-story.html

361 http://www.latimes.com/entertainment/movies/la-et-mn-oscars-2017-uta-immigration-
rally-20170224-story.html

362 http://www.vanityfair.com/hollywood/2017/02/uta-immigration-rally

363 http://www.latimes.com/entertainment/movies/la-et-mn-oscars-2017-uta-immigration-
rally-20170224-story.html

364 Months later, CNN cut ties with Aslan after he sent out profane anti-Trump tweets.
http://www.foxnews.com/entertainment/2017/06/09/cnn-cuts-ties-with-reza-aslan-
following-anti-trump-tweets.html; See also
http://money.cnn.com/2017/06/09/media/cnn-reza-aslan-decision/index.html;
http://variety.com/2017/tv/news/cnn-reza-aslan-donald-trump-1202460352/

365 http://www.latimes.com/entertainment/movies/la-et-mn-oscars-2017-uta-immigration-
rally-20170224-story.html

366 See generally, http://www.latimes.com/entertainment/movies/la-et-mn-oscars-2017-uta-
immigration-rally-20170224-story.html

367 https://inews.co.uk/essentials/culture/film/thousands-attend-free-london-screening-
iranian-film-trump-oscars-protest/

368 https://inews.co.uk/essentials/culture/film/thousands-attend-free-london-screening-
iranian-film-trump-oscars-protest/

369 https://inews.co.uk/essentials/culture/film/thousands-attend-free-london-screening-
iranian-film-trump-oscars-protest/

370 http://insider.foxnews.com/2017/02/24/robert-davi-oscars-actors-invite-illegal-immigrants-refugees-hollywood

371 http://www.businessinsider.com/actress-ashley-judd-womens-march-on-washington-2017-1

372 See http://www.radiotimes.com/news/2017-02-25/foreign-language-oscar-nominees-write-an-open-letter-against-the-climate-of-fanaticism-in-america; See also http://www.hollywoodreporter.com/news/oscars-foreign-language-film-nominees-condemn-climate-fanaticism-nationalism-979787

373 See, e.g., http://www.cnn.com/2017/01/29/opinions/trump-ban-xenophobia-disguise-amanullah/index.html

374 http://www.nationalreview.com/article/440539/democrats-first-grade-refugee-policy; See also

http://www.theblaze.com/news/2017/02/07/trump-immigrant-ban-protesters-asked-if-theyd-let-refugees-live-with-them-heres-how-they-respond/; See also https://www.infowars.com/video-liberals-support-bringing-in-refugees-then-refuse-to-house-any-refugees/

375 See Chapter 6, "Unity Productions Foundation," subsection on "Muslims and Screen and Television for more information on "MOST."

376 http://campaign.r20.constantcontact.com/render?m=1101291766794&ca=2870d3f2-99b2-43a3-ae83-faa48045cf6e

377 http://www.mostresource.org/storybank/most-hosts-hollywood-iftar/

378 http://campaign.r20.constantcontact.com/render?m=1101291766794&ca=2870d3f2-99b2-43a3-ae83-faa48045cf6e

379 http://www.arabamerica.com/events/hollywood-iftar-ramadan-dinner/

380 See generally http://www.mostresource.org/storybank/most-hosts-hollywood-iftar/

381 See, e.g., http://www.frontpagemag.com/fpm/170455/e-tracking-saudi-women-deborah-weiss

382 See Weiss, Deborah, The Organization of Islamic Cooperation's Jihad on Free Speech, pp. 16, 30-31.

383 http://www.arabamerica.com/events/hollywood-iftar-ramadan-dinner/

384 http://campaign.r20.constantcontact.com/render?m=1101291766794&ca=2870d3f2-99b2-43a3-ae83-faa48045cf6e

385 http://www.frontpagemag.com/fpm/263111/ramadan-month-jihad-robert-spencer

386 See generally http://campaign.r20.constantcontact.com/render?m=1101291766794&ca=2870d3f2-99b2-43a3-ae83-faa48045cf6e

387 https://islamqa.info/en/20327

388 http://campaign.r20.constantcontact.com/render?m=1101291766794&ca=2870d3f2-99b2-43a3-ae83-faa48045cf6e

389 http://campaign.r20.constantcontact.com/render?m=1101291766794&ca=2870d3f2-99b2-43a3-ae83-faa48045cf6e

390 http://campaign.r20.constantcontact.com/render?m=1101291766794&ca=2870d3f2-99b2-43a3-ae83-faa48045cf6e

391 See https://townhall.com/columnists/calebparke/2017/04/19/allahu-akbar-vs-god-is-great-ap-got-it-wrong-and-why-it-matters-n2315288

392 http://campaign.r20.constantcontact.com/render?m=1101291766794&ca=
2870d3f2-99b2-43a3-ae83-faa48045cf6e

393 http://www.gainpeace.com/index.php?option=com_content&view=article&id
=75:islam-the-religion-of-all-prophets&catid=34:what-is-islam&Itemid=107; See also
http://www.fiqhcouncil.org/node/8

394 S. Solomon and E. Alamaqdisi, "The Mosque Exposed," (ANM Press, 2007), p.8.

395 http://campaign.r20.constantcontact.com/render?m=1101291766794&ca=
2870d3f2-99b2-43a3-ae83-faa48045cf6e Generally, when one uses the word "but," what
follows the "but" negates what preceded it.
http://www.framingthedialogue.com/archives/everything-before-but-is-bull/

396 http://campaign.r20.constantcontact.com/render?m=1101291766794&ca=
2870d3f2-99b2-43a3-ae83-faa48045cf6e

397 http://campaign.r20.constantcontact.com/render?m=1101291766794&ca=
2870d3f2-99b2-43a3-ae83-faa48045cf6e

398 See http://www.wnd.com/2009/04/94847/; See also
http://archive.frontpagemag.com/readArticle.aspx?ARTID=34723

399 http://www.discoverthenetworks.org/viewSubCategory.asp?id=291

400 See, e.g, http://www.foxnews.com/politics/2012/09/05/democrats-restore-references-to-
god-jerusalem-in-platform.html
See also http://www.nytimes.com/2016/06/10/opinion/israels-problem-with-the-
democratic-party.html?_r=0

401 See, e.g., http://archive.frontpagemag.com/readArticle.aspx?ARTID=14999; See generally,
http://archive.frontpagemag.com/readArticle.aspx?ARTID=34970

402 See https://www.middleeastmonitor.com/20140329-israeli-apartheid-week-takes-us-
campuses-by-storm/

403 See, e.g, http://www.adl.org/israel-international/anti-israel-activity/c/students-justice-
palestine.html#.VW4H_6JFB2Y

404 Those who purport to be "pro-Palestinian" are much more against Israel than they are for
"Palestinians," as many of their positions, (including boycott, divest and sanction) hurt
Palestinian and Israeli jobs much more than they help Palestinians. See, e.g.,
http://www.npr.org/sections/parallels/2016/03/27/471885452/when-500-
palestinians-lose-their-jobs-at-sodastream-whos-to-blame; See also
http://www.jpost.com/Opinion/The-World-From-Here-Europes-BDS-labeling-hurts-
Palestinians-not-Israelis-432607
https://www.forbes.com/sites/carriesheffield/2015/02/22/boycott-israel-movement-
stunts-the-palestinian-economy/#204d98d21648

405 http://www.cjnews.com/news/international/qa-with-kenneth-l-marcus-defining-anti-
zionism-as-anti-semitism; See also http://www.timesofisrael.com/pm-says-anti-israel-
sentiments-fueled-by-hatred-of-collective-jew/

406 http://www.americanthinker.com/articles/2009/02/hate_speech_at_san_
francisco_s.html

407 http://www.ips-dc.org/events/the-5th-annual-dc-palestinian-film-and-arts-festival/

408 http://archive.frontpagemag.com/readArticle.aspx?ARTID=14999

409 See, e.g., http://yenra.com/muslim-film-festival/

410 See, e.g., http://greatlakesfilmfest.com/, See also http://en.kazan-mfmk.com/about-mfmk

411 See e.g., http://mmfilmfest.com/about/ Note: Da'wa is defined as an invitation to join Islam, evangelizing or pro-Islam propaganda. ACLJ, *Shari'ah Law*, p. 13.

412 See, e.g., http://www.themosquers.com/submit/

413 See e.g., http://www.aljazeera.com/news/2016/05/gaza-red-carpet-event-mirrors-cannes-film-festival-160513182023454.html

414 "Ummah" is the broader Islamic community.

415 http://www.aicongress.org/boston-center/new-england-council/muslim-film-festival/

416 See http://mmfilmfest.com/2016-films/

417 See generally https://www.theguardian.com/world/2017/jul/13/omar-khadr-settlement-canada-trudeau . The law suit was settled for 10.5 million Canadian dollars, which is approximately 8 million U.S. dollars.

418 See http://mmfilmfest.com/2016-films/

419 http://mmfilmfest.com/2016-films/

420 http://mmfilmfest.com/2016-films/

421 http://mmfilmfest.com/2016-films/

422 http://mmfilmfest.com/sponsors/

423 http://www.isna.net/film-festival.html

424 http://www.isna.net/uploads/1/5/7/4/15744382/film_festival_registration_form_2016__1.pdf

425 http://www.isna.net/film-festival.html ; See https://www.youtube.com/watch?v=X_alnGMBrxs

426 http://www.investigativeproject.org/mosques/409/masjid-at-taqwa

427 https://www.youtube.com/watch?v=X_alnGMBrxs

428 To the contrary, blasphemy laws create an environment that increases violence. See http://www.humanrightsfirst.org/wp-content/uploads/Blasphemy_Cases.pdf

429 http://caamedia.org/blog/2015/11/06/caams-muslim-youth-voices-films-coming-to-philadelphia/

430 http://yenra.com/muslim-film-festival/

431 http://www.themosquers.com/festival-history/

432 See https://www.investigativeproject.org/documents/20-an-explanatory-memorandum-on-the-general.pdf , p.4 of 18 within the text.

433 See generally http://shariahthethreat.org/debunking-the-myth-of-a-growing-trend-in-muslim-victimization/; See also http://www.danielpipes.org/358/are-muslim-americans-victimized; See also http://humanevents.com/2011/01/04/are-muslims-being-victimized-in-america-today/

434 See http://www.biography.com/people/chris-kyle

435 http://www.frontpagemag.com/fpm/256298/muslim-students-associations-petition-cancel-jeffrey-herf

436 http://variety.com/2015/film/news/box-office-american-sniper-shatters-records-with-90-2-million-weekend-1201408252/

437 http://www.huffingtonpost.com/2015/03/08/american-sniper-highest-grossing-movie_n_6827212.html

438 http://www.boxofficemojo.com/movies/?id=americansniper.htm; See also http://christianaction.org/news/2015/4/14/ny-college-postpones-showing-of-sniper-film-to-appease-angry-muslims

439 http://www.esquire.com/entertainment/movies/reviews/a31732/american-sniper-box-office/

440 http://www.businessinsider.com/american-sniper-highest-grossing-us-film-of-2014-2015-3

441 See http://www.imdb.com/title/tt2179136/awards

442 http://www.frontpagemag.com/fpm/256298/muslim-students-associations-petition-cancel-jeffrey-herf

Also http://www.foxnews.com/opinion/2015/04/23/university-maryland-cancels-american-sniper-after-muslim-students-complain.html

443 http://www.frontpagemag.com/fpm/256298/muslim-students-associations-petition-cancel-jeffrey-herf

444 http://www.frontpagemag.com/fpm/256298/muslim-students-associations-petition-cancel-jeffrey-herf

445 http://www.campusreform.org/?ID=6446

446 http://www.campusreform.org/?ID=6446

447 http://www.campusreform.org/?ID=6446

448 http://qpolitical.com/muslims-learn-why-you-just-dont-tell-clint-eastwood-what-to-do-this-is-epic/

449 See e.g., http://www.christianaction.org/news/2015/4/14/ny-college-postpones-showing-of-sniper-film-to-appease-angry-muslims; See also http://www.csmonitor.com/USA/USA-Update/2015/0414/Colleges-wrestle-with-screening-American-Sniper

450 http://www.sonypictures.com/movies/zerodarkthirty/

451 See http://www.imdb.com/title/tt1790885/

452 See http://www.imdb.com/title/tt1790885/awards

453 http://www.newsmax.com/Newsmax-Tv/james-woolsey-waterboarding-train-navy/2016/03/23/id/720570/

454 See http://www.progressive.org/news/2013/02/181013/hollywood-protest-against-zero-dark-thirty. It should be noted that the true historical story portrayed by the film should be told to the public, regardless of one's political views on enhanced interrogation techniques.

455 See https://www.theguardian.com/film/2013/jan/18/zero-dark-thirty-us-election

456 See http://www.frontpagemag.com/fpm/172092/suppressing-zero-dark-thirty-mark-tapson

457 See http://www.islamist-watch.org/blog/2013/08/in-hollywood-it-deja-vu-all-over-again

458 Tzu, Sun, *The Art of War*, https://suntzusaid.com/artofwar.pdf, p. 11, para. 18.

459 https://www.congress.gov/bill/114th-congress/senate-bill/2230/text

460 https://www.youtube.com/watch?v=SDouNtnR_IA

461 https://www.investigativeproject.org/2100/cairs-hollywood-crusade

462 https://www.investigativeproject.org/2100/cairs-hollywood-crusade

463 See generally https://www.investigativeproject.org/documents/20-an-explanatory-memorandum-on-the-general.pdf